THINGS YOUR MOTHER NEVER TOLD YOU...

MARION McGILVARY

Kyle Cathie Limited

First published in Great Britain in 2001 by
Kyle Cathie Limited
122 Arlington Road
London NW1 7HP
general.enquiries@kyle-cathie.com
www.kylecathie.com

ISBN 1 85626 407 6

Project editor Caroline Taggart
Designed by Button Design Company
Illustrations by Veronica Wood
Production by Lorraine Baird and Sha Huxtable

Marion McGilvary is hereby identified as the author of this work in accordance with
Section 77 of the Copyright, Designs and Patents Act 1988.

A Cataloguing in Publication record for this title is available from the British Library.

Printed in Singapore by Kyodo Printing Co Pte Ltd

Contents

Acknowledgements

With thanks to all the people who reached the parts my mother left untouched: Caroline, Kyle and all at Kyle Cathie for good humour and good sense; Nina for her endless encouragement and enthusiasm; Annie, Penny and Sandra at *The Times* who pay me money, say nice things and return my phone calls – the ideal relationship – and goddess Julia Cuthbertson at the *FT* who allows me to lunch and fund my shoe habit. More thanks to Julia Hobsbawm who talked me up and pushed me on, as did Sue Norris, Louise Chunn and Maureen Mills. Thanks to Judith, to Joyce for all her good-humoured toil and Rosalie for telling me all the things my mother didn't. Thanks to Harry Ritchie for being a good dinner companion.

And to all three and a half of my friends, past and present, who've sat around, supported me and laughed politely at my jokes. You know who you are. And you know who you aren't.

Finally, thanks to my sister Lesley and endless thanks to my mother for merely shaking her head and saying 'Oh, oor Marion' at my worst excesses, and to Mr K for everything, especially the children, who – if they're reading this now – would be advised to tidy up their bloody bedrooms.

Some of the material which appears in this book previously appeared in a different form in *The Times* newspaper, *Traveller* and *Prospect* magazine. The piece about a friend on a pedestal which appears on page 91 originally appeared in *Woman's Journal*.

Introduction

My mother told me zip. I left home aged 17 with no idea how the washing machine worked and only the haziest notion of how food arrived on the table (the only use I had for the gas stove was lighting cigarettes, eyebrows and long trailing collars on it – which admittedly, I did learn from her). On sex education her advice was 'to keep your hand on your ha'penny' – not terribly useful since, coming from Scotland, a race of supposed misers, I merely thought it meant that one should always keep one's purse snapped closed. And I didn't do that either.

She didn't tell me that I'd spend half my life worrying about effective birth control and the other half – post failed birth control – silently doing Kegel exercises trying to rebuild what has been hopelessly lost. Ah, pregnancy – the gift that keeps on giving. If only men knew when we get that far-off look of intense concentration that makes us look like contemplative Madonnas in the oddest of places – whether sitting at traffic lights, mid sneeze at a dinner party, doing jumping jacks in the gym or when we suddenly stop laughing in full flow, as it were – that we are not experiencing inner peace, but earnestly contracting and relaxing inner muscles in a place where the sun don't shine. And yes, strength and flexibility of the pelvic floor is a useful skill for gripping sex (I bet you mother didn't tell you that, either), but it's a lot more useful when you're running for a bus.

Of course, everyone tells you that you're going to turn into your mother, and everyone swears that, like death and dentures, this may happen to other women, but never to them. But given

5

time, gravity and grandchildren, it will. Accept the inevitable. One day your own daughter, the little person whom you love, cherish and adore, is going to grow up and find you as much of an irritation as you do your own mother. One day you'll hear your mother's voice speaking from your mouth, saying, 'Tidy your room.' One day you'll buy big pants, flat shoes and a foot spa. One day you may even embrace madness and start saving little scraps of soap.

To be fair, my mother probably did tell me lots of things, I just never bothered to listen. In common with most daughters, I was born knowing everything – a trait my own children have inherited. When I was writing this book, I showed my own teenage daughter the parts on friendship and life. But sex? What do you think I am – out of my maternal brain? Some things have to wait until she's older - at least 35 or 40 – when, frankly, I'll be so old I'll probably need reminding myself. And embarrassing sexual innuendo will be the least of my problems. By then, surely, we'll be back to death and dentures.

Life and How to Live it

Ponytails and other tall stories...

Hair stylists just don't speak the same language as the rest of us. Oh yes, they look like us (sort of), they dress like us, they even use the same words, but – don't be deceived – they hail from the distant planet Salon and they don't understand a single word you say.

How else do you explain the haircut from hell? You go in clutching a photograph torn from Blind Optimist's Hair Monthly. You have a long consultation with the Artistic Director – who is usually bald. You explain in minute detail what you want him to do. He nods. And then does exactly the opposite.

Okay, I know – you can't expect the poor stylist to create Jennifer Aniston trophy hair out of three colours red, major split ends and the remains of a home perm, but some sort of mutual understanding about the meaning of the word length might be a good start. How many times have you see a woman walking, wide-eyed, down the street, obviously in shock – perhaps trembling, with tracks of recent tears and a tendency to cover her head and flinch? Only the bounce, gloss and condition of her curls, with perhaps a faint whiff of mousse, will alert you to the fact that she's suffering from Post Traumatic Hair-stress Syndrome.

But we never learn. Still, we arrive at the salon full of hope and leave full of hair spray. You walk in, tossing your precious long tresses like Rapunzel, ask for an inch off the bottom, then watch wordlessly as the stylist throws down your hair – to the floor, in coils around your feet. Alternatively, you tell the stylist to crop and layer it, and she proceeds to take forty-five minutes to snip an eighth of an inch from the bottom with the precision of an eye surgeon.

Then there's the colour thing. Most hairstylists are functionally colour blind. They work on a whole different spectrum from the rest of us where copper means ginger and black means blue. They rely on shade books with little tufts of synthetic hair mounted inside like fishing flies; and from this you're supposed to decide how it's going to look on your head. Descriptions don't usually help. With names like Golden Bay, Amber Sunrise and Caribbean Sunset you could be forgiven for thinking you're choosing a holiday destination, not a hair colour. At least Optimistic Brown sounds honest, though I would be deeply worried by Intriguing Black – of all the things you want your hair colour to be – an enigma isn't one of them. And as for Happy Honey – well you probably won't be.

Whichever Pigmy's scalp you point at, the colourist will undoubtedly suck in her cheeks, look at your skin and say,'Oh we'd have to warm it up, tone it down, highlight it, lowlight it,' or some other Salonesque colloquialism; all of which mean 'fiddle around with foil until your head looks like an electricity substation' and/or 'add peroxide'.

One of my aunts, a woman of extreme fussiness who thinks genetic make-up comes in a Chanel compact, gave me this tip: cut off a lock of your daughter's baby hair and keep it, not for sentiment, but for the much more serious business of colour matching later in life. However, on this basis I would have three curls at the front, like a Mohican in Carmen rollers, and be pure white.

Colourwise, this is becoming pretty accurate as I grow older resulting in more roots than Arthur Haley. Over the years I've sported a variety of shades ranging from Hooker Yellow, Bar-Room

8

Blonde, Henna Halo Red and a very peculiar mortician's shade of black that should be called It's a Mistake – Don't Do It. But then, maybe I just make bad choices. Even on my wedding day – I arranged to have my hair done by a top stylist and took the matter seriously enough to go in beforehand for a discussion. On the day, however, the stylist had a hangover and didn't turn up, leaving me at the tender mercies of a trainee with stripes painted on her face, wearing a sailor suit (it was 1979) who obviously had not completed her earth assimilation course and had missed cutting, pinning and speech. She could only grunt and comb. I finally ran home, stuck my head under the shower and was still furiously drying my hair upstairs when the wedding celebrant arrived.

It's small wonder that we have been colonised by an alien race intent on conquering our curls – we act like willing victims in our own bad hair day and as a result deserve every back-combed coiffure we get. For a start – have you looked at your hairdresser lately? Who in their right mind asks a bloke with purple spikes along the crown of his head to give them a page boy? And how confident can you be that the blonde with deliberately dark roots, really understands the notion of 'natural' colour? This is before we even get to the legions of Salonese who populate suburban salons everywhere, quietly taking over the world by turning out an army of identically tinted, helmet-haired perms. Just don't even go there.

Meanwhile, we're gowned up and anaesthetised, deeply conditioned to accept anything. Why else do we lose the facility of speech once seated in the chair? Why else do we watch them scrunching the hair we wanted smoothed with a mounting sense of horror, but totally unable to say we don't like it? Recently, fancying myself with one of those casual, pinned-up, half-falling-down styles, I spent an hour in a mini face-lift with rollers pulled so tight I had eyes in the back of my head and came out of the dryer with my hair in elaborate sausage rolls. Then the stylist danced around like a magician's assistant with a mirror to show me the back, as though I really gave a damn what the rear of my head looked like when I already hated the front, while I said nothing but a weak 'lovely'. Transpose this to bad sex – do you compliment the man who has just spent two hours fancifully imagining that you have an erogenous zone somewhere near your navel, say thank you and pay him for the pleasure? Do you go back two weeks later and do it all again? I think not.

So why aren't we spritzing these creatures with their own firm-hold styling spray? What is it that turns a perfectly normal aggressive female into a meek monosyllabic mouse at the sight of a stylist with a pair of scissors? I blame it on the head massage. No sooner are you sitting down in front of the mirror than, even before you can even recoil at the unflattering overhead lighting, they're at you. Their fingers are running through your hair, fondling the ends, lifting and separating, doing the dry shampoo – the Salon equivalent of a dry hump.

'What are we doing today?' they murmur softly, and you can forget everything except your chequebook – you're mere styling putty in their hands. It's like love – you long to believe in the fantasy that this time it will be better, that this will be the one. That if only you submit to this dominant person brandishing a very large can of long-lasting, high-performance, firm-hold mousse, then the perfect haircut can be yours. Suddenly growing out the Meg Ryan easy-care messy look in favour of a sleek bob which requires daily blow-drying and torture by tongs seems only common sense. As my richer than God friend Judith who has been going to her hair stylist Louis for sixteen years, says, 'I don't choose my hairstyle, Louis does. I don't even choose the colour – when Louis says it's time for a change, then hey – I'm a redhead. I just do what I'm told.'

And it's true – a good hairdresser can get you to agree to anything – tax fraud, bondage or even a third child – though if he's gay he probably won't offer to father it for you. They wield power that other men, mere mortals such as husbands and lovers, can only envy. If my husband told me how to do my hair I'd spray him dead, but a man with an oversized comb in his pocket, his fingers rifling through my hair as though it was silk underwear and I'm on my back with my head in the sink before you can say 'extra body'. Plus, you get to kiss him afterwards, and he always tells you that you look fabulous, darling, which is more than most lovers do.

So, top tips for heavenly hair:

Never choose a hairdresser who can afford a better vacation than you can Since the chances are you're going to be stuck in that chair hearing about the stylist's holidays until pigs can not only fly, but always travel business class; it's deeply irritating to hear them banging on about Venezuela or their overland hike through China when all you've managed is a weekend at a shopping outlet village or an overnight stay at Granny's nursing home. Trust me, no matter how much you dress it up she'll know it wasn't a spa.

Never choose a hairdresser who is too starry Do you want a prat who spends most of the time boasting about the film shoot they've just styled – that's if they don't cancel you at the last moment for a music video? No, no, no – if you can't impress your stylists with your fascinating job in lightbulb telesales, who else can you bore?

Don't judge your hairdresser by the state of their own hair… because they always look a mess. Look at the other clients. Do you aspire to be plump, blonde streaked with nails like razor clams? Yes? Then you're in the right place. And a word on the razor-clam fingernails – if you want to have your head feel as though it has been lathered up by Edward Scissorhands – make sure your shampooist doesn't sport a set of long acrylics. I confess – I've never seen the point of spatula-sized fake fingernails – but I felt it.

and finally:

Once you have found one – never let him go Some women I
know have had their hairdressers longer than their husbands. Just as
you don't share your husband around your friends when their own
man isn't performing up to standard, nor should you ever willingly
divulge the name of your colourist or stylist. Failure to keep the code
of stylist silence will result in inability get an appointment with him
or her, ever again.

However, if you haven't been able to keep your big mouth
shut and have kissed and told the free world that your colourist is
a genius and are looking at a six-month time lapse before you
can get back for a root retouch – one further word of advice:

...do not let your mother do it Let her nowhere near your head
unless you have lice (believe me it's possible – read on, you naive
young thing) or she has a hand-signed certificate of excellence and
her own range of hair-care products featured on an infomercial.
Because, no matter what she thinks – she *really* can't cut hair. And
as for home colour – woman, are you mad?

Frankly, I wouldn't let her near my legs with a strip of hot
wax, either.

Primping – it's a dirty job, but someone has to do it

It used to be called vanity, but now it's just grooming.

Grooming is one of those things that monkeys do to each
other in public for free, but the modern woman is better advised to
either do it herself in private, or to pay a fortune to a stranger.
Facials, manicures, waxing, eye-lash plucking – after you've
passed the age of slumber parties and have survived the indignity
of having to draw your eyebrows after letting cross-eyed Linda
loose with the tweezers, just say no. Trust me – these things should
all be left to a trained professional.

My mother's generation hadn't the disposable income to
spend on grooming. Her beauty regime consisted of washing her

face, brushing her hair and wearing a clean pinny on top of the old one. I'm not sure she had sex either, since throughout my childhood, she repeatedly said, 'Oh Christ, Marion', so I'm sure I was an immaculate conception. The only beauty advice my mother ever gave me was to wash the back of my neck (presumably in case there's a hairdresser standing behind you holding a mirror) and never to shave my legs. 'Once you start,' she said, 'you're stuck doing it for the rest of your life'. But what else can you do? Except fall in love with a man who likes bear hairy women – which, if you ask me, is equally problematic.

According to Arab legend, the Queen of Sheba was rumoured to have such hairy legs that King Solomon constructed a special palace with a glass floor so he could look up her skirt and see them   on approval as it were. He then instructed his djinns to make her a special potion to get rid of the offending hair – the first depilatory. Given that the Queen of Sheba was supposedly fabulously wealthy and stunningly beautiful, it's a wonder she didn't tell him to pluck off. I guess, even then, Goddesses just didn't have body hair. So of course I ignored my mother's advice – though I did comply with the neck washing. I plucked, peeled, pruned and depilated until my body looked like an Amazonian deforestation project. If nothing else, it passed the time between hot dates, months with an R in them and most of my teens which, love-wise, was a very slow period. Yep, the baths, the potions, the scented oil, the hot wax, the eye-lash curlers – it's true to say that until I was twenty-one my major relationships were with a bottle of bubble bath and a bar of soap. Though I was very flighty and flirted indiscriminately with a lot of brands, all at the same time. What a waste – all that effort expended on a cup of instant coffee and an equally speedy man in patterned socks with a terrible handicap who thought foreplay was a golf stroke.

Feeling old is relative. Turning twenty you suddenly feel grown up and thirty seems ancient. Forty makes thirty seem young and fifty makes forty sound like a jolly good age to stick at. Sixty is one foot in the grave and the other at the chiropodist – until you get to seventy and suddenly you're counting your remaining friends on the fingers of one hand – which is fine because five is as far as you can get before you've forgotten why you were counting the first place. By the time you get to ninety most women have been dead for ten years – though some of us feel like it has been a lot longer than that.

No wonder we take comfort in lipstick. For most of us there are three major periods in life when grooming plays a major part:

Youth – when you don't need it
You fool, you're beautiful and you don't know it. It's not until you get past thirty that you realise that youth is the greatest beauty treatment life can offer.

Okay, I admit, there are strings – it's more of a free gift with three purchases that you don't really want – a kind of bonus to compensate for adolescent acne, puppy fat and teenage angst. Of course, you don't realise you're beautiful. You think that life mostly stinks and that it would only be bearable if your legs were thinner, your bottom didn't stick out and you didn't have a spot the size of Ohio in the middle of your forehead (though you're hazy about where Ohio actually is, while the spot has its own guidebook and hourly bus tours).

But it won't. I can't lie and say that it wouldn't be a teeny, teeny bit better, but believe me, inside every later-life beauty is an ugly kid who couldn't get a date in High School with anyone except the guy with sweaty hands – and even he didn't call you back. However, repeat after me: popular girls marry too early, have six babies and live hippy ever after, in trailers, watching game shows all day. Okay, now I am lying, but it's a helpful fantasy to believe in when you're sitting at home thinking that no one loves you.

I thought I was the ugly kid. I was gawky. I was tall. I was
skinny enough to be a supermodel, except that in the part of the
world where I grew up – wouldn't you know it – podge was
actually prized. Old guys, seeing me walk down the road with my
mother, would whistle at her. To this day I would rather do a
knickerless handstand than reveal to you my teenage nickname.
Confidence? I thought it was a ring you got from a tube of
toothpaste and I tirelessly tried to floss, gargle and brush my way
to owning one. It didn't work but I ended up with good periodontal
health even though I didn't manage to meet and marry Rod
Stewart. Yet another example of how life works out for the best?
What would you rather have – your own teeth or an old perma-
tanned guy who spends more time in the hairdressers than you do?

I think Sleeping Beauty had the right idea. The only thing to
do with adolescence is to go to bed for the duration – stay in
your bedroom, listen to depressing music and sit it out. That's why
teenagers sleep so much. But do not despise the booby prizes
handed out as destiny by the wicked fairy (forgive her – she was
probably menopausal). If all you got was youth's innocent bloom,
an inner glow, plump skin and sex appeal, we older women
would hunt you in packs and wear you as jewellery round our
spreading waists. Spots and self-consciousness are the price you
pay for being allowed to live. And they pass. No forty-something
woman worth her cellulite really envies her younger sister that
brief, melanoma-free moment in the sun. Life is like sushi – you're
on the conveyor belt and you're coming our way.

One day you'll yearn for the time when make-up was an
embellishment, not a form of camouflage. When a fine line was
one you crossed when you shared your boyfriend's toothbrush,
and not the beginning of the end of your face. Take a look at any
girl in any double-page spread in any magazine. Comeawn – it's
not the Bird's Eye's pea shade of her eye shadow that makes her
look fabulous – if you slapped that on in real life you'd look like
an extra in *Star Trek* and only an equally weird man from the
Starship *Enterprise* would ever dare beam you aboard. She's not

selling you this season's new colours – she's selling you youth – and you've already got that.

And anyway, there are no new colours. It's just the same old brown (green eye shadow – don't go there) – but in packaging. Nevertheless, you're going to do it. You're going to have your eyebrows waxed – and if you're totally off your tree you're going to spend two minutes every morning brushing them. You're going to cleanse, tone and moisturise. You're going sit around practising for death in a face mask (smile when it's set – this is your future). You're going to steam your skin, scrub it, buff it, peel it and purify your pores. Hell, girls, when did we all get so dirty?

It's an unspoken truth that many women think that only a pair of smooth heels and trimmed cuticles stand between them and a night of unbridled passion with the man of their dreams, but why does finding love mean continual body maintenance? Why are we in perpetual training for a full kit inspection before sex? Since when did 'be prepared' mean carry a condom and always shave your legs? Sadly, silky skin and a liberal application of body lotion will rarely transform any man from a fast frog into a slow prince. If anything it will only make the frog go even faster. Then before you know it, you're in love and suddenly, ten years down the line you've become...

Somewhat older – when you need all the help you can get

You're in your mid thirties, or beyond, and you've either got the man or you've taken him back for a refund and not found anything else you really like. Either way, unless you were lucky enough to have your store credit in your purse when the top-of-the-range merchandise was reduced, and you're happily wearing it out on every possible occasion, the chances are your man is hanging in the closet, washed out and a bit last season.

It doesn't mean you don't adore him – but really, what's love got to do with it? You do his laundry, you still desire him, when he's not on another continent, you aren't too tired, there isn't a child already in the bed, and you feel thin. In cosmetic terms he's the old brown, with the worn-down pencil stub – still your favourite shade, but God, how you long for something with a nice pointy lead and a whole lot of glitzy new packaging. And if you can't have that – then you'll buy a lipstick instead.

It's an irony that after spending most of your precious, peachy, pristine youth grooming your pert young body to ensure you have sex on tap, you eventually discover that when the tap is running, you're not terribly thirsty. This is when body maintenance begins in earnest.

Frankly sex is cheaper, but who actually does it anymore? An alarming number of married women don't have sex, they have facials. They have reiki and reflexology. They have personal trainers and cleaners and, occasionally, nannies. They have fake St Tropez tans because they are too busy for holidays. They have manicures as though holding an emery board had suddenly become a skilled occupation requiring a degree from the Suckers School of Nail Science. They have massages to relax them because, if you thought it was hard being a teenager the first time round, honey, it's a lot tougher when you're middle-aged.

You're probably about thirty-five when you take a proper look at what you thought were horrifically embarrassing photographs of yourself aged twenty, squinting into the sun, afraid to go topless because no one could tell whether you were on your front or your back, and scream – Hell, there was nothing wrong with me! I was gorgeous! I was a babe! Why were men not dropping at my feet like ice-cream wrappers?

Because they are all idiots, that's why – but never mind. Remember the trailer park? They saved you from yourself and the teenage pregnancy with the High School heart-throb who was going to get a beer gut and a temper, and leave you anyway.

The first object of my obsessional affection married my second best friend (she was my first, but – hey – things change). He would cross the street to avoid me and chose her instead. I was heartbroken for about – ooh – five years with time off for alternative disappointments. They were married by nineteen, divorced by twenty-five, and he was dead of an overdose by forty. If feeling gawky helped me avoid that life, then thank you God. I was already divorced myself when I discovered that my rear end, which I felt stuck out too much and was endlessly trying to cover with baggy clothes, was indeed my biggest asset and the reason why the students in the library kept asking me for books on very high shelves.

So now you're an older, wiser, strong, self-possessed, self-confident able woman who can, do and will – and what do you do? Why you spend all your energy trying to look like the girl you never appreciated while you had her so you can get the man you've already got and don't want any more.

It's probably even worse for the beauties who can't kiss their younger selves goodbye and are locked in a permanent arm wrestle with time. The plain Janes improve with age – look at Hillary Clinton or Cher (okay she had some surgical help, but whatever gets you through your forties), while the breathtaking beauties – say Cybill Shepherd or Marianne Faithfull – just age, sliding into it like a car on a slow ice skid. Or in Marianne's case, a head-on collision.

What you're left with is moisturiser, good lighting and walking out of rooms backwards. So after that too brief hiatus when familiarity with your partner has lulled you into a false sense of hirsute security, you're back to the razor – big time. And this time you're playing with the big boys.

We've already talked about the hairdressers, but now you're also having your nails done by a Vietnamese woman (who thankfully can't speak much English and isn't interested in your holidays – so don't talk about your cruise – it's tactless) who's wearing a white coat trying to convince everyone that she's a medic. Though, visiting the manicurist is more like visiting a hooker than a doctor – you have to pay up front before the service of your choice (French or straight hand job, with or without massage, plus extras like nail piercing) – though not in case you do a runner once satisfied but so you don't smudge your polish getting the money out of your purse.

Then you have a woman from Eastern Europe firing a hose of ice cold water at you maybe once a month to stimulate the lymphatic system, rolling you in seaweed till you look like the world's largest sushi to drain the lymphatic system, a masseuse pummelling you with sisal soaked in algae to tone the lymphatic system – but hands up who knows what their lymphatic system is. You don't bother much with waxing, instead you're having electricity conducted into your follicles and immolating your body hair, or you have it burnt off with a laser. You have a person who dyes and shapes your eyebrows or applies a semi permanent colour to your lashes which you have permed and extended. Another who squeezes your blackheads. You have pedicures. You spend half the time ridding your body of toxins, then have Botulism injected into your face and call it Botox so it doesn't frighten you into frowning again. You have collagen injected into your lips so you can pout your way through EMA – early middle age – thus co-ordinating your facial expression with your general mood. You take fat out of your thighs and inject it in your cheeks. Why, if you're mad and have money you can have every part of your body trimmed and tucked, including your labia – imagine that conversation: 'Hmm – yes, it's a bit untidy, we'll just take an inch off the ends.'

It's not pampering – it's busy work for the bored and bonkless. It's what you do instead of heavy petting with a visit to the spa as the ultimate release – the orgSpasm. Here you find more white coats, more therapists masquerading as psychiatric nurses, small curtained rooms, soothing music, long quiet corridors and women in rubber shoes – have you died and gone to heaven or a horrifyingly expensive lunatic asylum? Is it pampering or anaesthesia?

Who has enough time or energy left for sex, or the opportunity to find someone to appreciate your newly frilled and hemmed labia properly when they spend all their free time being petted like an expensive pedigree cat at the beauty parlour? This is before we even get to the gym. But don't worry – we're going there later.

By all means, we should look our best, for the good of our soul and our own well-being, but enough – all this worry about eternally youthful skin when, face it with a magnifying mirror, that bus has left the station with a one-way ticket to tortoise wrinkles and osteoporosis. You can take the scenic route – but either way – you're not coming back.

So use a sun block and avoid the sun like syphilis anyway. Take calcium. Have an early night. Make love, not Max Factor. Because no matter how fabulous you look, the clock is ticking. Eventually you'll be sitting in the rest home for glamorous geriatric grannies looking at the third stage of good grooming – wishing you had spent less time sloughing off dead skin and more time snogging.

Old age, when you're beyond help My feeling here is that you should forget skin tone and just aim for bladder control. There are no men around anyway because they're all dead, or flirting (true to type) with the young floozy of 82 who wakes up every morning, applies some bright red lipstick (from memory) and smokes a cigarette. I just hope that floozy is you.

Gym Slips

My mother's idea of exercise was pushing a vacuum cleaner round the house for half an hour each morning, followed, seasonally, by rug beating, step scrubbing and vigorous dusting. The idea of using any of her precious spare time to go to a small, airless room, perfumed with stale sweat and Eau de Jockstrap, to do it all again for fun would have been unthinkable. Let alone paying the membership fees. Imagine – knocking yourself out every day without even a spotless kitchen floor to show for your trouble. Stop the madness – is this why we liberated ourselves from housework?

Nevertheless, liberated we are, with the flabby muscles to show for it. In today's sedentary life, if you can still walk without a zimmer frame by the time you get to eighty then it's not from overzealous Hoovering – no doubt you have been building your bone density and exercising your muscles by going to the gym. At least, I assume that's why we put ourselves through the torture of regular exercise. I know there are those who actually enjoy it, but to me a work-out in the gym is like practising synchronised sex without a partner. Think about it – all that panting and sweating. The grunting and the groaning, the straining and the gasps of relief when you finally finish your stomach crunches. This is before we even get to the machinery which looks as though it has been designed by a sadistic gynaecologist.

'Can't you open your legs any wider than that?' asked a trainer in my gym recently. The last time a man asked me that question he had a copy of the Karma Sutra in one hand. However, in this case, I was sitting with my legs akimbo in a machine that purports to exercise your inner thigh muscles, but looked to me more like a medieval birthing chair. Why the hell do you need inner thigh muscles, I asked myself as I tried to squeeze my knees together. 'Harder, push harder,' he exhorted, which in most cases of physical exertion is usually my line.

Then there is the near naked physical proximity towards people you hardly know – a serial one-night stand, coupled with a sequence of repetitive bum lifts, hip thrusts, or doing it doggie style on the mats, head down, as if you were waiting to be penetrated by a World Federation Wrestling champ.

The big difference is, I hate the gym and only hate sex when other people are having it – such as when my girlfriends have brand new lovers and are having better sex than me. Three times a night. My idea of a visit to the gym is ten minutes on the rowing machine on which over the last ten years I have surely rowed far enough to have discovered America, and twenty minutes sitting on a bicycle soft pedalling my way through a good book. I usually take Gourmet magazine or the latest glossy cook book to have arrived on my doorstep – the pornography of the fat. Other women are pumping up the stairway to heavenly thighs, visualising themselves thinner, but I'm sitting on my bottom thinking about dessert. No change there, then.

In top-of-the-range gyms there are three different exercise rooms. The macho men's gym where the women go to strut; the women's gym, where the competitive women go to show off; and the mixed gym for the shy of both sexes. I do think that sport centres should actually pay people like me to go along – as encouragement to others. I must offer incredible comfort to the other lunging lumpies sweating it out on the treadmill like demented hamsters. It also makes the smug skinnies feel even better about themselves. My gym is full of beautiful people, mostly air-brushed mothers whose equally perfect children go to the same school as my daughter, the odd famous face and a whole row of unemployed actresses sitting on the bicycles reading Stage. Then there's me. There's the ignominy of going on the abdominiser after a five foot slip of a girl and having to take some weights off and it's equally demoralising to be struggling not to fall over on the treadmill next to someone who, in her head, is sprinting towards the finish line at the Olympics. She's there, hardly breaking a sweat, hair bouncing behind her like a Clairol ad and there I am, invariably right beside the air conditioning fan but nonetheless looking like I'm starring in a wet t-shirt competition, with hair all over my face like the wild woman of Borneo.

It's not a good look. I used to be one of the smug skinnies with my leg effortlessly bent behind my ears, smiling benignly at the plump and out of condition, thinking it's not exercise you need, it's liposuction. But now the running shoe is on the other foot and I'm the leaden wide-hipped straggler who should get a reward for bravery, just for turning up.

Reputedly exercise releases endorphins which produce a feeling of euphoria similar to that experienced after sex. This must explain why everyone leaves with a huge smile on their face, smoking a post prandial cigarette. Though, from experience, I'm more likely to slump on the floor, roll over and fall asleep. And I feel terribly virtuous, which you really shouldn't after sex. Well not if you've been doing it properly, and certainly not if you've been doing it with wrong person.

Gymetiquette

Don't say hello to anyone you know Wear a mask if necessary. Neighbourhood gyms are like neighbourhood restaurants – too close for comfort. If you greet everyone you recognise you risk having your business broadcast around the changing room faster than Demi Moore gets her kit off when it's artistically necessary. And everyone will talk about your cellulite. I know, I do.

Don't stand next to anyone Gym etiquette dictates that you should really leave a machine free between you and the next exerciser. Not only will you be out of their all-important odour zone – or if it's a man, his splash zone – but you will not feel inferior if they have their machine on a higher setting than you. Just as in the shower – it's very bad manners to look. The towels which are provided free by the gym may only be large enough to cover a gnat's backside, but are ideal for this form of modesty. I rarely sweat enough to need one, but it's very useful to cover the dials with. no one needs to know I'm walking backwards.

Join a gym where there's something to do apart from kill yourself Join one with a television to watch or people to laugh at. As I mentioned, I usually take something to read but before I discovered that I was multi-talented and could ride a bike and hold a book at the same time, I used to take a book on tape. This had its disadvantages – sometimes I got too involved in the voices in my earphones and startled fellow exercisers by yelling in horror during the gory war scenes in Pat Barker's *Regeneration*, and bursting into loud, inconsolable tears when another character died. At least the book with copious sex scenes resulted only in a lot of exceedingly fast, but silent, pedalling. Commenting on the plot might lead people into thinking you have a literary form of Tourette's syndrome, or that you're just plain mad.

Take talcum powder Real gymnasts put it on their hands to stop themselves slipping. Normal people use it to stop their thighs sticking together.

Don't sing Don't wear ear-phones and join in with the songs on the radio. Believe me, your voice doesn't sound quite as great as you imagine it does in your head.

Clothing If you have only recently started exercising please do not rush out and buy yourself a whole new wardrobe. Yes, lycra is useful for flattening flab, but it won't work miracles. There's something about going to the gym that brings out the ballerina in those individuals who remind you of the dancing hippos in Fantasia. There they are doing stretching exercises in their high-leg leotards while apparently oblivious to the fact that half their bottom is hanging out the back. And that's just the men, who also wear their cycling shorts so tight that you can tell whether or not they've been circumcised. In my gym there's a rule that men must wear shirts with sleeves (though no jacket and tie – yet), lest we are offended by the sight of hairy armpits or drenched in their rain forest microclimate. I wish they'd pass a similar rule that women over fifty should not wear crop tops.

So wait a while before going full on with the exhibitionist gear. However, there is no point in going in your anorak. There are some women in my gym wearing so much kit that if they had a compass they could scale the north face of the Eiger. Then all they do is a few gentle yoga exercises before taking a short stroll to the water fountain.

A final word here on the wearing of sportswear outside the gym. The reason they're called sweats is that you are supposed to engage in some activity that encourages perspiration. Running for a bus in a pair of warm-up pants and trainers may well raise the heart rate, but it's not exactly exercise – and there's a worrying trend amongst the overweight to use these garments as day wear. Just because they are loose, baggy, have elasticated waists and fit you, does not mean you are fooling passers-by into thinking you do anything more strenuous than tying your shoe laces. Remember, in America leisure rhymes with seizure and lolling around in jumbo joggers profits no one except the cardiologist. Similarly, men in Polyester soccer shirts, whose greatest manoeuvring skill is in tucking their trousers underneath their beer bellies, are to be avoided.

Yoga is a great alternative to strenuous exercise. involving lots of muscle strengthening stretches, deep breathing and the occasional snore when someone gets too relaxed and falls asleep. However, yoga, with its myriad of postures, just like energetic sex, should be undertaken in a darkened room or in the company of other people to whom you are lovingly committed. In my yoga class I used to suffer badly from posture envy, not being able to get even my legs off the floor while everyone else was standing on their heads. Then I saw my friend Suzie, looking at herself in the floor-length mirror, suddenly stand up and go rushing out the door. The reason – well, have you seen your face upside down recently? This is one reason why women over a certain age don't get on top during sex with quite the same alacrity as they once did. Look at your breasts when you lie on your side. If they don't move to the side then you're either full of silicone, flat-chested, or under 40. Your face has the same propensity to fall to the side, as poor Suzie discovered. As she had recently started an affair with a much younger man, she was suddenly aware that this lopsided, collapsing face was the same one she presented to her lover every night in bed.

The fast lane to love – they say that gyms are great places for meeting men which, given that you've already seen each other at your worst with next to no clothes on, is possibly true. There are a lot of gorgeous men in my gym who I would be happy to do bench presses with, but unfortunately they seem to be more interested in checking out each other's six pack than in my bouncing pecs. However, do give the his'n'hers gym visits a miss – please. Have pity on the rest of us. It's bad enough having to watch couples smooch all over each others in coffee shops without having to watch them hold hands on the stairmaster. Simultaneous sweating is something you should really do in private.

Spring-clean your life

As I mentioned earlier, my mother only ever broke into a sweat over housework, and spring had another, more ominous purpose beyond that of planting up the window-box with bulbs and the semi-sacred festival of the chocolate egg. The minute spring was sprung she was into her work-out clothes – overall and duster – and down came the curtains, up went the ladders and she got down on their knees and scrubbed up for the annual spring clean.

My mother was the undisputed queen of clean. I swear her hobby was dusting. I would come home from school and find the house transformed. Literally – it would take five minutes to realise I wasn't in the wrong house. Being the daughter of a secret furniture shifter meant that sometimes I'd discover my bed in a different

room, the sofa banished to the dining room, and the dining table transported to the lounge. Our television set moved around the walls like the points of a compass and if the fireplace had been on wheels she would have moved that too. Every item in the house would have been buffed and polished with Pledge – I had the cleanest apples in the whole class. The downside of all this frenzied activity was that for hours no one was allowed to sit down in case we messed the place up again. If she could have hung me on a hanger and put me away tidily in a closet, I would have been shut in the coat cupboard all through adolescence.

So my mother certainly instilled in me a healthy respect for cleanliness, but unfortunately, for most of my adult life I've harboured an equal disrespect for doing anything to attain it.

Throughout the years when my mother regimented the cushions into rows by yelling at them like a sergeant major, and spent hours rubbing up the top brasses or inspecting the sinks, I was always hiding in another room. On the first days of spring, she'd be dragging hearth rugs out on to the lawn to shampoo them, or attacking the bathroom tiles with religious zeal and a small toothbrush, while the only thing I beat was a hasty retreat elsewhere. I didn't really have a sulky adolescence, I just kept my mouth shut and avoided eye contact so she wouldn't give me any chores. Even now, although I organise obsessively, alphabetise my cosmetics and colour co-ordinate all my drawing pencils, I am not about to get into an antiseptic lather about it like that woman on an American TV ad who invites passers-by to smell her toilet. Just kiss my S bend, honey, and get a life. When I worry about a flush, it's going to be a hot one.

Who are these advertisers selling to – or is it true that now we've got the Cold War sorted, we're lying awake at night worrying about waxing our floors? Do they think we believe that you really do get Cheer and Comfort from laundry goods or that the one thing in life you can Depend on is an incontinence pad – never mind that Poise is pretty much impossible when you're peeing in your pants. When a friend from an ad agency asked me how he should spin his latest account for an anti-static floor cloth, I told him he was asking the wrong hausfrau. I'd spin it like a Frisbee, darling – right out the window, and straight into the bin.

But what no one told me as I watched my mother dash around like a Stepford wife on speed, was that though the cleaning gene may lie latent for most of your youth and young adulthood, one day you wake up and are more worried about the wrinkles on your sheets than on your forehead. Frankly, I still don't give much of a damn about dirt. To me dust is like debt – as it accumulates it becomes less noticeable. Another fiver here or there on the already crushing overdraft isn't going to matter much. No matter how many deposits you make at the National Bank of Idleness, dust is a lot easier to service than debt. I see no point in trying to get rid of it in small doses – I let it pile up and clear it all at once.

My big problem is mess. I hate it like poison. I have an aversion to chaos, clutter and scatter cushions, and I can't stand once-worn, crumpled clothes half-falling off the hanger and sixteen towels in a heap on the bathroom floor. The moment I had a place of my own my immunity to disorder wore off and I came down with a bad case of the tidy virus, which I am helpless to resist. Yes, I too became a closet clean-freak. I don't want to come out of it with a mop in my hand, but I sure as hell want to cram everything back in there.

Thankfully, as well as teaching me 101 useless things to do with liquid detergent, my mother also taught me the sisterly secrets of Zen housework – namely, concealment.

- **Firstly – the gentle art of paper folding**   I was 21 before I realised that newspapers and magazines did not automatically live underneath the sofa cushions until the pile grew too large to balance on. Only when I'd inadvertently turfed my boyfriend's mother off the chaise longue whilst looking for the television listings did I discover that some people threw their old newspapers out. Now there's a novel idea.

- **Secondly – Japanese litter arrangement...** in which dishwashers are ideal for storing away yesterday's breakfast cereal bowls, laundry baskets useful for anything you can't be bothered to hang up, and attics and basements perfect for hoarding all those shoes you bought in the 1980s that just might come back into fashion.

Like me, my mother never threw anything away. Unlike me, everything she kept was carefully and beautifully stored – as if the secret drawer police were likely to make a dawn inspection without warning.

Tallboys were not lanky pre-teens but a treasure trove of clothes being kept 'for best'. Actually, we had whole rooms kept for best. A best front bedroom and a best front sitting room for visitors who never came, a best front lobby connected to the best front door through which the visitors who never came could make their arrival and, of course, cupboards full of best china on which the best visitors would never eat. So naturally, best clothes were absolutely necessary. Sandwiched between these was a stash of savings books which she secreted in strange places around the house with the frugality of a squirrel storing nuts for the winter. They were everywhere: Premium bonds and insurance policies. Endowments and savings bonds. Stuffed inside teapots and biscuit tins, held together by shrivelled elastic bands.

She also liked to keep some new clothes aside to be buried in just in case death should call unexpectedly, without ringing first. However, not content with maybe a nice nightie and a clean set of underwear, my mother seemed to regard death as a two-week holiday in Blackpool. She had whole wardrobes of burial clothes – a costume for every occasion. She could go to her maker dressed for whatever heaven had to offer – whether a cocktail party or a walking tour of the Hebrides – she was going to be the best dressed corpse in the graveyard. And her accessories would always match.

I have the opposite problem. I keep clothes for worst – old leggings for the gardening I never get round to, and overalls for the decorating I will never undertake. But at least all the jumble is artfully arranged.

• **Thirdly – harmonise your surroundings** I like the thought of a minimalist home where everything is bare, spare, white and pristine. But I also like clutter and primary colours – no doubt a result of never having received a nursery education and experiencing enough play with sand, water and building blocks. So organised chaos is the only solution. Hats on hooks rather than decorating the lampshades, CDs collected on a rack and books – never in alphabetical order – but at least put on the shelves facing the same way up. If you have a spare room, hanging your clothes behind the door transforms it into a dressing room; old letters, odd bits of paper and a calculator makes it an office; torn newspapers and the ugly books which clash with your colour scheme make it a study, or – if you throw your husband's shoes in there as well – his study.

• **Fourthly – unburden yourself of worldly goods** If in doubt, throw it out. Sadly, this mantra doesn't really work for me. I may pretend that the dead flowers are indeed dried, that crushed clothes the last word in deconstructed chic, and that my eclectic mix of odd glasses and mismatched plates is in fact a collection, but we all know the horrid truth. I'm a slob who wouldn't know spray-on starch from a complex carbohydrate. I change my hair colour but not my curtains and don't give a hoot about clean windows or germs hiding underneath my toilet bowl – as long as they have the good sense to hide, I'm not going to seek them out. I just don't want my mess to be untidy.

• **And lastly – serenity** Minimalism certainly simplifies life for the slovenly so embrace your dark, dingy side and lighten up. Invest in a lot of drawers and walk-in wardrobes, remain calm and just don't open the cupboard doors. Ever.

Life would be bliss if only I could have one of those people who you see in airports and hotel lobbies walking about with a dustpan and brush in one hand and a mop in the other. They could just follow me around like a whiff of expensive perfume, shake and vac away my cares, pick up the debris in my wake and carry my luggage. They're called cleaners. Do yourself a favour and hire one.

My mother, however, is beyond help. Yes, she too has finally agreed to have a cleaner, but she vacuums and dusts before the woman arrives. And then she offers her afternoon tea.

Chars begin at home

The domestic help issue was a difficult one for both of us to come to terms with. Fashionable as it may be to wear one's working class origins draped around one's neck like costume jewellery, sometimes the faux pearl necklace pulls a little tight. I come from a long line of household help. My great-grandfather worked in the stables, my grandmother was a cook, and several of my long-dead aunts worked as maids for the local nouveau riche. It was like a Barbara Taylor Bradford novel, but without any of the royalties. Subsequently, I can't say anyone in my family was comfortable being the employee. I felt it was exploitative, degrading and deeply offensive to pay someone else to do your dirty work.

Twenty years and four children later, I eat my words with extra hypocrisy and a big helping of double standards on the side. The minute I had too much to do and not enough time to sit on my own sanctimonious backside, I climbed down from the moral high ground, compromised my principles and became a serial employer of nannies, au pairs, gardeners, cleaners, handymen, caterers, a visiting masseuse, and a much, much, happier person. I discovered my true calling in life – I was not born to clean, I was born to delegate.

It would be fine to say that while embracing domestic help with all the fervour of a born-again Christian at a fundamentalist rally I have been doing something much more important than sorting the herbal tea bags according to their ingredients, like – say – running the Department of Trade and Industry. But, the truth is, once freed from household drudgery I dicked around doing a lot of equally mundane jobs from which I earned barely enough after taxes to pay for the help.

While the au pair stayed with the baby, I worked as a secretary for a woman married to a life peer. I spent my time, not typing, but doing her shopping whilst continually tugging my forelock and calling her Lady Whatserface. Given the important administrative job of writing out her Christmas cards, she told me snippily that I had to be more careful – I had made a mistake with Lady Twitt who should, actually, be addressed as 'The' Lady Twitt.

'Is there a difference?' I asked. 'Indeed, Marilyn,' she said with frosty hauteur, handing me the social register and telling me to mug up on the social etiquette required when addressing the aristocracy. I replied by saying that, while we were on the subject of proper forms of address, I thought it would be nice, if, after several months spent in her ladyship's employment licking her ladyship's envelopes, she might bother to remember my name.

So, the facts don't change. There can be little dignity in working in a subservient position whether it's in a public restroom, an office or a stately home. The difference is in the way you are treated. Be good to yourself and better to anyone who works for you. Okay, taking the au pair breakfast in bed is carrying the tea-tray a bit too far, unless he's 24, East European and looks like Goran Visjnic, and then I'd say – go for it. But remember, there are sexual harassment laws.

These days the problem isn't agonising over the morality of employing a cleaner – it's holding on to the one you have. None last more than two years with at least six months sick leave before they eventually fire you – usually on the basis that your house is too difficult for them to manage. Well you know that – isn't this why you needed help with it in the first place? Doubtless this is why my mother cleans her house from top to bottom before her cleaner arrives. The woman, after all, has a bad back and can't do much. You wouldn't want to offend her. God forbid – she might leave.

Cleaners don't like housework any more than the rest of us – nor do they like your teenagers, your cat hair, your ashtrays, your record collection or your stairs. They don't like the fact that you only get terrestrial channels and they can't sit down and watch their favourite Spanish soap opera beamed over by satellite. They don't do toilets, or bathrooms, anything higher than chest height or lower than the waist. They won't dust because of their asthma or wash floors because they're allergic to ammonia. They don't like small children and they think your vibrator is for buffing up the silver – or you assume that's why they have a duster wrapped round it as they walk around the house.

They also talk about you with their other clients which is why it's a very good idea not to employ the same cleaner as your neighbour or anyone with whom you don't wish to share the contents of your husband's Swedish film collection. So if you don't want to air your dirty linen in public – then don't employ someone else to wash it.

Cooking the books

In the seventies, Scotland was not exactly a Mecca of culinary sophistication. We pretty much ate anything as long as it was brown and boiled. It was meat and two veg, usually cabbage, turnip or – as a seasonal treat – hard Brussels sprouts which tasted and looked like sheep droppings. Our diet was so limited that until I was seventeen I thought baked beans were a green vegetable. Red pepper was only available dried like fish food into dandruff-sized flakes and sold in a box, garlic was scarcer than a vampire at a dawn solstice, and I didn't see an avocado until I was in my twenties, when I promptly spat it out.

My mother didn't teach me how to cook. Without the leisure for extended mother and daughter pastry play sessions, cooking was just another chore, and one which she managed faster alone.

Nevertheless, we did forge a relationship over food. Until she hung her pinny up aged seventy-nine and went on a food strike, my mother was a brilliant plain cook, but a forgetful one. Once a week or so she would go to work, having risen at the crack of dawn to make beds, hoover, and plump cushions, come back home in her lunch hour to prepare the evening meal and then leave the house, forgetting to turn off the gas under the simmering stew. I would then get a frantic call at school to race straight home, turn off the stove, air out the kitchen and hide the burnt pot at the bottom of the garden in the compost heap before my father got in and yelled at her. Now if you fear your significant other would respond in a similar fashion should you single-handedly attempt to keep the home fires washed, cleaned, polished, stoked and burning – and yet fail to have cooked the little sweetheart a meal – here is

Tip number one – tell him to bugger off Those days have gone, buddy, and we're all dancing around the ashes. My mother was a martyr to the goddess housewife, but I certainly am not lighting any candles at the particular shrine. Oh no – when other kids learned the secrets of superb sauces, and salad tossing at their mother's knee, I learned kitchen solidarity, how to redeem a scorched saucepan and a deep, unspoken conviction that in my own home – I'd never hide a saucepan.

But tip two – should you need it... is that adding some clothes detergent to a pot and boiling it up will remove the most stubborn carbonised deposits, though God knows what it does to your insides at the same time – bleach, brighten and smell like a summer breeze, probably – but if you start coughing up bubbles, I'd suggest maybe just throw it out.

Eventually I taught myself to cook from books and even went to professional classes to learn how to make the fiddly things. Not that this was always an unmitigated success. Being somewhat divorced from food preparation (opening a tin was my one skill) I hadn't fully appreciated that chickens didn't joint and skin themselves and that fish fillets came with heads, bones, skin and eyes which turned reproachfully opaque after five minutes under the grill. But I manage. I can transform a burnt stew into fantastic gravy (just don't scrape the burnt bits off the bottom of the pot). I can bake a cake, boil a lobster, roast a joint – heck, I can do it all and juggle at the same time. I've also had my own share of disasters; the rice that I washed down the sink and blocked the drain; the casserole I dropped on the floor and served anyway; the coq au vin for Muslim relatives who, of course, don't drink; the boudin blanc I gave to vegetarians, telling them it was an egg-based meatless sausage; and the bulgur salad I prepared for people who wouldn't eat wheat. My take on this is that people shouldn't be so bloody picky in the first place, that ignorance is bliss and alcohol evaporates. I admit it – I regularly lie about my ingredients. Amongst my favourite phrases are:

- Oh you don't eat dairy – really, how interesting – no, there's absolutely no butter in this – I used olive oil.
- I made it myself.
- Yes, it's organic.

I have great sympathy for vegans, the lactose intolerant, wheat-free freaks and vegetarians – indeed I gave birth to one – but it doesn't half drive me nuts when I invite people round for a meal

and discover that instead of having a dinner party, I'm running a restaurant devoted to their special needs. Food is a gift, one lovingly prepared to give warmth, succour and pleasure to others and it's bloody irritating when no one eats what you've cooked because – oops I forgot to tell you – I don't eat salt. So, seriously, for the sake of your health, I would not advise anyone to eat at my house if they have a serious peanut allergy unless they have an accompanying letter from their doctor to prove it.

So tip three – before you begin... check your guests' dietary requirements and decide whether you like them enough to be bothered. And if you can't be bothered, then...

Tip four – get a bloke to do it for you Cooking can be an art, but most of the time it's merely an achievable skill for people who don't have anything else much to excel at – that's why men are so good at it. Women are trained from birth to offer five meals a day, but men like to show off their culinary skill with 'serious cooking', which means they do it once a week when there are guests to applaud. Apparently all a man has to do is walk into the kitchen, grill some tuna, chop some herbs, cut up a few baguettes and hey – he's walking on water (but definitely not using it to wash up) – Jesus of the kitchen doing his loaves and fishes bit for the multitude (you and the cat). But remember – the price you pay for invoking the kitchen god is a high one. You will have to bear his insufferable smugness and smile weakly when guests congratulate you on your good luck, as though the man had single-handedly saved the world in his lunch-hour instead of just poached eggs and whisked up a hollandaise sauce. When did you last hear someone congratulate a man because his wife made a good dinner? Oh, I do get so tired of the trophy cook. Why the bloody hell shouldn't men cook? – it's not like you need to have breasts in order to produce food. They're cooking, not lactating.

And don't even get me started on barbecuing. At even a hint of sunshine all males seem to want to get in touch with their inner neanderthal – as though cave man first looked at fire and thought, mmm – marinated steaks and Louisiana hot sauce. Two days into summer there he is in his apron, a sausage in one hand and a pair of tongs in the other, being the chef de charcoal.

But look – charring meat is not cooking. There is no art to burning food. You don't need to trundle out the barbecue, scrub down the grill, clear out the ashes, dead beetles and families of snails from last summer and turn the house upside down for a box of matches. You simply put some oil in a frying pan and walk away and leave it. As my mother proved – it's easy.

However, since the barbie draws men forth like members of a Zoroastrian fire-worshipping sect, just let them get on with it.

Tip number five – when barbecuing is inevitable Add beer and scatter napkins liberally (otherwise they may wipe their mouths on your tablecloth). Do not stir – agitating may result in an outbreak of bad temper. Leave unattended until meat is thoroughly black and eat only salad. This way, at least they are the ones who will get splattered with fat, breathe in the carcinogenic fumes and smell of rancid smoke for the next five days.

If you are intent on hitching up with a trophy cook then, galling as it may be, try to find one who does it properly:

Tip number six – do not attempt to ride the one-trick pony

We've all met the guy who 'does a great stir fry' or 'a wicked curry' – or in other words you're acting impressed over a man whose accomplishment is a high chilli pepper tolerance, who cooks the kind of thing a woman knocks up every day of her life without being canonised for it. The first man who ever cooked for me was an American Rhodes scholar called Dan. He claimed to do great Chinese food and invited me round to his rooms in Oxford to sample it. The food arrived – rice, noodles and hamburger meat – just thrown on a plate and sprinkled with soya sauce – the resulting gloop covered with a transparent film of uncooked egg white.

If this is what I have to eat to get laid, I thought to myself, looking at the awful mess, then frankly, Dan – a skinny, befreckled, red-haired geek – though bright, wasn't that much of a babe.

'What's this stuff?' I asked, picking up a tangle of green leaves he had scattered on the top. 'Oh, I don't know,' he replied, 'I found it growing in the college grounds and just threw it in.' My appetite and my libido both vanished quicker than a stripper in a snowstorm. At a loss what to do with the stuff, I ladled it into my make-up bag when he wasn't looking and left quickly thereafter. I just hope he didn't find the bit I left hidden in the soil of his Swiss cheese plant.

Actually, I am married to a man who can cook. Even better, he can make packed lunches, pour breakfast cereal, wash salads, chop vegetables and do the clearing up. I am a happy woman. I can live without competition in the kitchen – as long as I have help. I enjoy cooking oh – say at least once a month; the rest of the time I just do it because I love food. I love bad food – fat, crisp fried potatoes that you wear on your hips like an ugly accessory; cream, butter, French full-fat saucy food, rich stews, runny cheeses, calorific desserts, pastry, pasta and polenta. And since you've got to eat to stay alive, you might as well embrace the preparation of it, otherwise you're going to be bored and discontented a lot of the time. And hungry.

Alternatively...

Tip number seven – you can visit a lot of restaurants Now, food used to be something you ate, but nowadays it's a passion, a crusade, a whole belief system – the cult of Foodism. And everyone is a foodie, chattering around their dining-room tables about outlandish ingredients as though they got points for naming ten kinds of salad leaves. Being food literate is as important as knowing who won the Nobel Peace Prize and infinitely more pertinent than who will win the next election. We all have to be able to source our ingredients and discuss the provenance of the beef. Supermarkets, after being touted as the answer to a busy woman's prayers, are now verboten. Get thee back to the corner gourmet store, woman, and know your onions from your shallots. Your mushrooms may be ceps, girolles or morels, but never magic – and when you talk about your dealer you don't mean the man who huddles by the door after a late-night phone call, you just mean the chap who sells you cheese. But shopping well is extremely time consuming. Only those who do it professionally, 1950s housewives like my mother, or migrant farm workers can spend all day hand-picking olives. And I'll be damned if, after years of blood, sweat and gravy, someone is going to walk into my kitchen and judge me on the quality and brand of my first-pressing virgin olive oil.

Entertaining has become a trial by dinner party, cookbooks are not manuals but big double page spreads of gastroporn to be gloated over and television cooks are now bigger personalities than pop stars. They don't just sell us recipes – they sell us lifestyle. But please remember that television cooks are not busy housewives running to the supermarket after a hard day at the office like the rest of us. They have food economists who test their recipes beforehand and kitchen assistants who do the vegetables, and clear up the sets for the before and after shots. And when it all goes wrong, they still hide their pots, although this time from the camera, not a disapproving spouse.

Television cooks have people who shop, people who chop and people to mop their brows and redo their make-up between shoots. They are not preparing a quick supper for six close friends in time snatched from the rest of their life. This is their life. So:

Tip number eight – do not feel guilty Most people do not have colour-supplement lives and there is no need to sit there weeping into your canned soup just because you don't have a stainless steel kitchen with professional cookware, wall-to-wall shelving, a chrome magimix and a cupboard stocked with fresh vanilla pods, sixteen varieties of rice and handmade pasta sold in a tissue-lined coffin. Get a life, not a lifestyle. No matter how many fancy gadgets you have, you're only making yourself something to eat – not splitting the bloody atom.

What's even more ironic is that most of the people gracing our screens obsessing about food apparently don't seem to eat any of it. While out in the real world, the rest of us are on a permanent diet.

Slimming – how to look great, feel miserable and starve yourself slim

Gluttony may be a sin, but starving yourself to fashion-model thinness is a curse we could all happily live without. It's not that I have any objection to owning a pair of thin thighs myself, it's just that I'm not prepared to eat corrugated cardboard spread with artificially sweetened wallpaper paste to get them. I eat for a living – and okay, no one forces me to help myself to the pre-dinner canapés, the extra glass of champagne, the bread, the butter, the hors d'oeuvres, three further courses, a pudding and the chocolate truffles that come with the coffee. I could just suck in my cheeks and take a few bites. I always plan it that way – you know – they'I'll just order plain grilled fish and pass on the wine' pledge that you make when you're on the way to the restaurant. But somehow, once I get there, my self-control is always in another handbag, and I gaily eat the lot. As a result, in the land where men worship fat-bottomed women, I will be Queen and anyone who wants to challenge me will have to kiss my dimpled royal orb and sceptre.

But although it's politically correct to defend the right of the individual to live it large and wear their love handles with pride – there's a difference between upholstering your bottom with a comfortable amount of padding and having more cushions than a lawn set, complete with a canopied swing. Truly fat people are not jolly, especially when you've just asked them when their baby's due – three months after it started college. Even worse when you discover you've just asked a man. It is no walk in the park being overweight – it's a slow, puffing, out-of-breath struggle round the clearly marked footpaths with a rest for an ice cream and a chocolate milk shake.

No one can pretend that cellulite is a sign of beauty. Given that nothing in my wardrobe without an elastic waist actually fits me any more – I know what it's like to be driving round and round fat town thinking that it's a place I really don't want to visit. I'd much rather be a refugee seeking sanctuary in Skinny City. I have the directions, I just don't fancy the uphill struggle.

However, over in Thinsville, it's not much better. The skinny are miserable too – they just have nicer clothes.

Obey the calorie code Your mother and others, usually rather plump people, will tell you that diets don't work. This is a lie. Of course they do. But dieting comes with its own guidebooks – and its own very peculiar customs. Bookshop shelves are heaving with tracts urging us to find physical enlightenment between the diet

sheets – the Hay Diet, the Adkins Diet, the Blood Group Diet –
even one that advocates 'living on light'. They all work if you stick
to them (except the one which involves eating nothing but light
bulbs) – but all will have you chewing your own arm off with
boredom, if not hunger.

And if it's not bad enough feeding those of your friends
who have food fads, then just wait until they are slimming and
start laying down the diet law according to whatever guru they
happen to be following. If they're food combining, for instance,
they avoid eating carbohydrates and proteins in the same
meal. In this way it takes them three days to eat a
cheeseburger – on day one you eat the bun, on day two you
get the meat, and on day three you get the cheese. All you
need for this diet is a long memory and you can almost
convince yourself you're eating proper meals. Carbohydrates
without protein may encourage weight loss, but it's a bit like
going on honeymoon without your husband – there's clearly
something missing.

**Taking to the empty road – or abstinence makes the tart grow
fonder** Abstinence is the cornerstone of dieting. You don't have
butter on your toast. You don't even have the toast. You drink your
tea (always, always herbal) black or green, your milk is fat free,
and your cola full of chemicals such as aspartamene and
saccharine that, like love, offer sweetness with a bitter after taste.
Everything from your cottage cheese to your mayonnaise is lite,
but you probably aren't. Join the club – neither am I.

My fridge is full of pots and packages all guaranteed to be
low in fat while my cupboards are crammed with food that is high
in fibre, cholesterol free and with less than half the calories of
something else that tastes a hell of a lot nicer. Then there are the
yolkless omelettes, the sugar-free jams, dairy substitutes full of
hydrogenised vegetable oil, air, more air and emulsifiers to bind it
all together, and the virtually fat-free yoghurt that tastes like hair
conditioner without providing the healthy shine. The cream I rub

into my handbag probably has more taste. I'm sure the reason so many women's cosmetics smell sweetly of coconut and fruit is because we are all half-starved. The nearest thing we get to a sugar fix is licking off our strawberry lip gloss, and the only whipped cream we allow is the stuff in a jar that we spread on our wrinkles.

Having forsaken so many of life's pleasures, if we took a vow of silence we could all join a holy order of penitent nuns – The Sisters of Slim. Except there's no point in getting thin just to cover yourself up in a hassock.

Common phrases for negotiating your way through temptation

There's a whole world of women's fridges out there similarly stocked with slimming food. These are the ladies who lunch on a chicken Caesar salad (hold the chicken, the dressing and the croutons) accompanied by a glass of still mineral water. And then what do they do? Why, they have two bowls of French fries and a side order of mayonnaise to dip them in, follow it with crème brûlée and then refuse coffee because the restaurant doesn't have skimmed milk. This is what abstinence results in – excess followed by lunacy. You also invent a whole new vocabulary for the simple business of eating:

• **Being good** In diet language this does not mean polishing your halo and helping old ladies across the road, whilst simultaneously knitting woollen squares for Romanian orphans. Being good means eating only food with the same consistency, and half the flavour, of carpet underlay. It means throwing the chocolates you got for Easter straight into the bin without even removing the cellophane, weighing your daily 2 oz allowance of cheese and strictly following all food guidelines as laid down by your particular diet.

Of course, if you do this for any prolonged period you become so deprived that you lose the place altogether and...

• **Slip** Not an embarrassing fall on an icy slidewalk or a necessary undergarment for those who wear a skirt without knickers, but becoming so depressed on your diet of citrus fruit and Chinese herbs that you start eating everything in sight that isn't tied down.

• **Being naughty** In slim speak this means eating the whole box of chocolates on the way to the bin, eating cereal straight from the packet, demolishing the peanuts that come with the drink you weren't going to have, and finishing your own and everyone else's dessert. Now, after a week of starvation, I call this understandable, not deviant. I save naughty for the really big things like knocking men out so I can eat their Mars Bar and running over pedestrians at traffic lights because I'm suffering from food rage.

• **Wicked** Anything tasty made with sugar, butter and cream, especially chocolate – often received with girlish sighs, gasps and squeals of delight more befitting unexpected under-table foreplay from Antonio Banderas.

• **I shouldn't** What you say before tucking into anything 'wicked' – except the Antonio Banderas option, when you should merely say thank you.

• **A treat** Antonio telling you he loves you fat and wants to have your babies, or anything your diet allows you in the way of a calorie controlled dessert – for instance a rice cake spread with peanut butter and then scraped off again, or one lick of ice cream.

• **A delicious shake** A revolting powdered drink you have instead of food.

• **It doesn't count** Nothing counts if you eat it from someone else's plate, if you eat it standing up, between meals or under the influence of alcohol, which is why so many diets fail to have the promised results. Then there's the endless plea bargaining when you say to yourself – well I missed breakfast so I can eat this bag of crisps – it doesn't really count, and if I skip lunch, I can have two glasses of wine and a pudding instead. It's a highly sophisticated form of madness where we all behave like inmates in the same asylum.

• **I'll just have coffee** This is what your friend says in a cafe just after you've ordered a bagel, a danish, a cranberry muffin, or all three, usually delivered to the very cute waiter with a self-satisfied air of smugness. What she's really saying is – 'unlike pig-face here, I have the self-control of a porn star, I'm too sophisticated for refined sugar, and think hunger is a country somewhere in the Eastern bloc'. And if she smokes, she's saying it with an implied French accent.

No self respecting dieter can live without coffee. Not only is it a stimulant and an appetite-suppressant, it also signals to the world just how terribly, terribly overwrought, stressed and 24/7 busy you are. It adds an edge of suffering to a diet. A woman on the edge of starvation just has to get her caffeine fix before she can function – a badge de guerre, a trophy to the rigours of her very important life and the rigours of dieting. Coffee is to the modern urban woman what alcohol and cigarettes are to the front line war correspondent – proof of battle fatigue.

Other phrases with much the same meaning are: 'I can't get through the day without seventeen double espressos,' and 'Oh darling, I simply live on caffeine'. And all are usually accompanied by a bad case of coffee shakes which they possibly imagine is a form of aerobic exercise.

• **No – Yes** Well, it is a common phrase in my case. I've never figured out how to say no when I really want to say yes, yes, yes. I didn't always have this problem – as a kid I was a picky eater. Pasta hadn't yet been invented in Scotland, other than the slimy kind that looks like fishing tackle and comes in a can with tomato sauce, and rice was a pudding with a skin thicker than a politician's. I didn't like potatoes. I ate a naturally carbohydrate-free diet with the help of the table drawer where I hid everything I hated, then waited until the coast, or the kitchen, was clear – and I could come back and bin it.

Nowadays this would be called an eating disorder. So many of our eating habits are dysfunctional that I wonder how much hunger has to do with what actually goes into our mouths. We eat when we're bored, we eat when we're sad, we eat whenever we happen to be passing the fridge just because it's there – and when the time comes to sit down for a convivial meal, we're racked with guilt and can't eat. Currently I seem to be suffering from a bizarre form of bulimia where I binge eat, but don't throw up afterwards, and a reverse anorexia where I am overweight but look in the mirror and, despite all evidence to the contrary, still think I'm thin. It's only when I try to slip between parked cars when crossing the road and get stuck that I realise the awful truth – the person living in my head is not the same one who is living in my body. Having to be cut free by the fire-brigade can really dent your self-image. As well as the car.

Dealing with unfriendly natives in Thinsville

If you eat next to nothing, count calories, watch your fat intake and persevere with a diet then of course you will get thinner – though I do advise against the lunching on light approach unless you want to glow in the dark. But be warned, the skinnies are just as miserable and food-obsessed as you are. The only thing that will change is your dress size. You will be in a constant state of anxiety about gaining it all again and, if your body ratio remains the same, you will still think you have big hips/thighs/breasts or – for the really neurotic – ankles. You may shed pounds, but you will also shed many of your friends who are consumed with jealousy at your newly svelte silhouette – especially if they're still wearing elasticated polyester fat pants and tunic tops to hide the bulges. I know, I am that friend.

Go along to a slimming club and if you've lost a few pounds at the weigh-in, 'Loser of the week is Tracy – down 5lb from last week' will get you a round of half-hearted applause. Elsewhere, however, the appropriate mode of address amongst women is the friendly greeting, 'Oh, you've lost weight, I hate you.'

And the thin who are welcoming to visitors and say things like, 'Oh, you've lost weight, you look fantastic' are really saying, 'Hell, you were fat and ugly before.' And if they say this when you haven't lost weight, then you know that the last time you saw them you looked even fatter.

My theory is that there is only so much fat in the world. It's like the water supply, it's just endlessly recycled. So when someone close to you loses weight you can be sure that somewhere else, someone else is gaining it . Beware thin friends – you might be catching their excess pounds. If only by comparison – you're definitely going to look large.

However, there are four diets that require no self-denial, no self-control, some of which even gain you sympathy from your sisters in size:

The Stress Diet Divorce, splitting up from your boyfriend, moving house, death of a loved one or the traumatic discovery that your scales have been broken for months, combined with accidentally seeing your reflection in a shop window can all induce rapid loss of appetite, weight and occasionally hair loss – an unwelcome side effect, but it does grow back. As do the hips. Unfortunately, when life starts to be hunky dory once again, your appetite will return rested and ready to work against you. But at least it's a start.

The Sex Diet Falling in love, discovering hitherto unknown heights of sexual frequency and athleticism, and obsessive stalking can result in massive calorie burning (following your loved one round the country and calling every hour requires immense stamina) as well as increased cardio-vascular health, low back pain, carpet burns and calluses on your knees. When combined with the Stress Diet after it all goes wrong and you start finding text messages for the wrong athlete on your phone, it works well, providing you don't take solace in tubs of Haagen Daz which, television sitcoms decree, you must eat in bed whilst wearing his old t-shirt and singing 'Only Women Bleed'.

The Jealousy Diet Again, another useful diet, especially in conjunction with the Stress Diet. Jealousy is virtual lyposuction. Cosmetic surgery for the mind. It rips you apart and leaves no scars. And if you are suitably consumed by it you will have no room left for pudding. Though be warned – it also eats up your insides and leaves you very, very bitter.

The Third World Diet This is a more costly diet and involves travelling to the Indian subcontinent, Central Africa or the Middle East and eating only fly-ridden food from street pedlars. Alternatively you can visit a lot of bad restaurants and hope for the best. Dangers are that this diet can involve a hospital stay (which will enhance the effects) or mortal illness, which can be fatal. However, at least you'll be thin when you pitch up in front of your maker and thereby guarantee yourself a place in Skinny Heaven where all the beautiful people spend eternity filing their nails and wishing they had eaten more pizza while they still had the chance. The Third World Diet also can involve a great tan, a lot of nice photographs and some wonderful 'when I was back-packing though Bolivia/in jail in Afghanistan'-type stories, ideal for dinner parties once you're able to digest solid food again. Do not mix the above diet with drugs of any sort, otherwise you may be very thin, but you will also be inside a Thai prison with no one to admire you except the prison guards.

If all these fail, then my current favourite involves getting rid of any mirror too large to fit inside your handbag – a dental scope is ideal. You don't need a full-length mirror to see if your bum looks big in your new stretch pants – your bum looks big because it is big. It's a design fault. But you should also avoid all reflective surfaces, especially those like kettles and toasters which will distort your image and make you look deformed as well as huge.

I call this the ostrich diet, but for God's sake, don't go sticking your head in the sand – or your bottom will be in the air.

And denial, I'm afraid, only works so far.

The Pursuit of Happiness

What do women want?

When I was growing up, my mother's desires were simple –
more sleep and white goods. My mother was one of the first
women to have it all – a full-time job, a family, a house to run
and a husband who expected a meal on the table every night.
She was a hardworking casualty of the fifties, still Hoovering
under the illusion that men wore
the trousers and women had to
make do with an apron and a
vodka martini. All she wanted,
apart from another three years in
bed, was a range of labour-
saving devices. She wanted
washing machines and
fridge/freezers; an oven with
an eye-level grill so we could
see whatever was burning
more clearly, and a revolving

spit that we might have dried socks on before anyone thought of cooking on it.

So apart from instilling in me a deep love of material goods and a healthy respect for my own salary, she didn't offer many clues as to what was supposed to make me happy. Nevertheless, I do know what I want. It's just that it changes every day and the only thing I'm absolutely sure of is that, whatever it is, it isn't anything I already have.

When I was single I longed for marriage. When I was married I longed for half the student bodies in the college where I worked. When I graduated from seducing students I wanted another husband, kids, cats and a Sports Utility Vehicle. And now that I am deep in happy, ongoing domesticity, I often dream of a life of wanton singledom and last-gasp promiscuity – just as long as I can keep my husband. And the house. The walk-in American fridge. And the children – though on the kids I'm willing to compromise.

If we are to believe Hollywood, then according to the film *What Women Want*, all we really desire is a leathery, past-his-sell-by-date, prune-faced Mel Gibson, miraculously able to read our minds. We girls sit around at home with our legs crossed, wishing on a film star, and hope for a touchy-feely guy to keep us company when we're lonely, help us pick out our clothes and offer love advice. I don't think so. Isn't that what gay men are for? Give me Mad Max any day.

When it comes to love, for something that offers unconditional adoration, warmth and affection, and doesn't give a damn what you're worrying about – you're better off with a cat. At least you only have to feed it once a day and you don't have to do its laundry.

Who wants some patronising bloke trying to get in touch with your feelings? Personally, I'd be happy if they got in touch with basic female anatomy, and where the kettle is (amongst other things). I want a guy who will make me a cup of coffee, pick up something for dinner which doesn't involve pricking the plastic film five minutes before it goes ping, and never, ever say, 'I know what you're thinking'.

Otherwise, what I want – what I really, really want – are accessories.

Four little objects of material desire

The Cinderella complex – keep the shoes and screw the prince

When I saw that film, I didn't want Mel Gibson. I wanted Helen Hunt's red satin stilettos, or even the powder-blue spike heels – though she can keep the matching slim-line frock. It would never fit. Accessories, however, always fit. When the bottom drops out of your world, or your jeans, you can hide behind your handbag. When you're feeling flat you can elevate your mood, and elongate your calves, simply by stepping into a pair of three-inch heels. You

can wrap yourself in a scarf, even when the jacket refuses to fasten and give yourself the velvet glove treatment – in pink, green and turquoise from good department stores everywhere.

If sex is shopping, then shoes and handbags are the two most important erogenous zones. Shoes are sex for legs. And while there are many of us in a happy, monogamous relationship with the simple black dress, the favourite coat, or the one must-have skirt or shirt of the season, when it comes to accessories we're promiscuous tarts. Shoes are like toyboys you fall in love with, even though you know they are totally unsuitable, too young, too tight and cost you too much money. Yes, you have the good old dependables waiting for you in the cupboard at home, but you can't resist a fling with the toe candy. And just as being in love makes you feel beautiful, when you wear those new shoes, suddenly you're sexy, glamorous – you're Helen of Troy in Mui Mui mules.

You fool yourself that they make you look thinner – though in my case I fear they merely make me look like the Amazon Queen in heels – but either way, you walk taller, with your spine arched, your shoulders back and your chest stuck out like you're going to balance a cup of tea on it. Well you have to, otherwise you fall over. They also make you walk incredibly slowly, a fact that men don't seem to appreciate as they stride down the road ahead of you while you totter after them (they probably don't notice – to them your natural place is three paces behind). But while heels improve your posture, navigating the sidewalk in them doesn't. Walking in high heels and watching where you're going are mutually incompatible activities. Who wants to track their slinky, megabuck footwear through puddles and city grime – or, let's be honest, over anything made of concrete, except possibly Paris or Milan.

Yelling 'Backup there Tonto, Jimmy Choos coming though!' doesn't exactly match the sophisticated sex-kitten image you are carrying in your head. Most definitely, fine shoes and thigh boots are not made for walking. They are dressing up for big girls.

Of course, with every lover, the shine wears off after a while. Eventually you look at the object of your affection and realise you have nothing to say to each other. What once looked cute now looks corny, and you are back out cruising the shoe shops looking for a replacement. Or two.

But don't:

Please, don't go to the ball in white shoes. American women, possibly by law, may not wear white shoes after Labor Day at the end of September. Sisters – why wait that long?

Unless you are a bride (or Cherie Blair), when footwear is the least of your problems, remember that anything more than a shade lighter than your skin tone will make your feet look bigger than Minnie Mouse on steroids. No woman needs that kind of anxiety – we have enough size issues as it is. Furthermore, white heels are tackier than a hooker's chewing gum.

Loafers, sneakers, trainers – fine – but if you want to go posh partying wearing jogging shoes and are planning on post-ball waltzing or vice versa, don't take the bloody things off without opening a window so the Prince can climb out.

Two watch words – foot deodorant.

Co-ordination. A friend of mine who makes all her own clothes (need I say more) once advised me that the secret to successful dressing was to choose your shoes and handbag to match your eyes. At this rate I'd be wearing muddy green/grey shoes and look as if I'd just walked through a swamp. And how would you get away with anything from Burberry unless you had very unusual brown check irises? For God's sake ignore that, especially if you've got a hangover. Red shoes are God's little gift to women with the heart of a tart (I got married in some second time round – though possibly the matching tights were a mistake) and people with Judy Garland fixations. I suppose there's nothing wrong with a matching bag – but co-ordinating with your bloodshot eyes is a bit much.

Don't wear slim-heeled, open-toed slinky sandals with jeans unless you also have an ankle bracelet, drive a Ford Camero, and are proud of both.

Don't wear two-tone court shoes whose toes look as though they've been dipped in chocolate. You may think you're Jackie Kennedy but you're either a suburban soccer mom or a member of the British royal family, and both identities should be hidden.

Avoid irony. Shoe irony is a test of your level of taste and discernment. We love silly shoes, but beware of absurdity. You know how it is – you see a pair of must haves – things you would have loved when you were twelve – possibly in green tartan made by Moschino, often in pink (appealing to those who haven't outgrown Barbie) designed by someone whose job it is to produce very ugly things and persuade you that they are 'fun' (exactly like Barbie).

They are not. They are expensive mistakes that, unless you are a children's entertainer and enjoy looking ridiculous, will haunt you for ever like the one-night stand with the chap who asked you for his cab fare home when you only had a fifty-pound note.

Frivolity is good, but fun is not a word you should associate with shoes, except when you've taken them off, preferably in a bedroom.

And incidentally, always let the bastard walk home afterwards. Never give men money after sex. The other way round is a matter between you and your conscience, though flowers would be more usual.

Look after the pretty ones. Some women keep their shoes in little felt shoe bags, stuff the toes with tissue paper and store them in their boxes with a mug shot to remind them of the contents. If you know a man who does this and are romantically interested in him, you are out of luck – he's gay. If you know a woman who does this, she almost certainly isn't. If you think the practice seems excessive, remember that if you leave them lying around they will start to mate and the bastard offspring look like ugly, mongrel creatures from the Island of Dr Scholl. On your own foot be it.

Sensible shoes. I know, you don't want to face it, but in this your mother was right. High heels will give you back problems, bunions, hammer toes and probably Ebola Fever for all I know. So, you must own some flat, comfortable footwear in which you can actually walk, if only to wear until you can change into the other, foxy pair which you're carrying in your handbag. This cuts down on the amount of time you have to suffer like the little mermaid, walking on knives. But for those of you still having trouble keeping up with Speedy Gonzales – currently in the restaurant while you're still getting out of the car – the real trick is to get him behind you. If you're doing it right, he should have no desire to do anything but watch you undulating ahead.

My mother's own choice of footwear didn't get much beyond slippers. Especially those with sheepskin lining and tassels on the front. Obviously I'm not following in her footsteps.

The bag lady If shoes are illicit flings which you have to keep quiet about, hiding them at the back of the closet hoping your husband won't notice, handbags are more like serial monogamy, with a few serious affairs on the side and a gay walker.

Even if you are lucky enough to have the rich husband of bags like a Kelly or a Fendi baguette, you still need an everyday Mary Poppins one-size-holds-all handyman – a bit of rough. Though rather than having a standard lamp and a parrot inside you're more likely to be carrying around that pair of flat frumpy shoes which I mentioned earlier.

Then you may have a couple of seasonal classics – a pastel leather this season, snakeskin last, ponyskin the one before. Additionally, perhaps there's an Anya Hindmarsh in printed plastic or a Lulu Guinness for your girlie moments and something special with sequins and feathers for the evenings (and that's just the man). The evening bag should only be large enough to hold a lipstick and the cab fare home (again, let me remind you – just your cab fare home).

However, as everyone who has ever played around will tell you, you must have a good memory to have an affair with a handbag. How else do you remember where you left your purse, your keys and your chequebook. Swapping everything over in the mornings takes hours.

I loathe, hate and detest classic handbags. The only thing they say about you is that they cost a lot of money – and money isn't style, it's pack following for people with no taste and sugar daddies. I like a handbag with enough personality to divert attention away from my stomach, or big enough that I can hide behind.

In practice this just means nothing black, nothing brown and very, very definitely nothing plastic. Instead I have bags in more shades than Maybelline has lipsticks which I can use to glam up even the most ordinary of outfits, working on the basis that if they notice the handbag, they might imagine that the safety pin holding my skirt together is me having a Liz Hurley moment, not a premenstrual day of bloating.

A handbag should be both beautiful and useful. A babe on the outside – a bomb site on the inside. A handbag is your inner slut. It's a place to hide the detritus of your slovenly life – curled up tissues, spare pants, a palm pilot, loose change and a single matchstick. A thing of beauty in which you can transport all manner of useless items, and which you can fumble through whenever you're nervous. This brings me to the old chestnut that a handbag is nothing but a vagina on a string. Well, I don't know about you, but I certainly don't do that when I'm feeling insecure and anxious. But should you feel the need – trust me – it's infinitely more socially acceptable, in public, to fiddle with your bag.

Anyway, it's rubbish. It's not big enough. Obviously we women are not walking around with a set of matching luggage between our thighs. What do they think is hidden there – the lost city of Atlantis? It's a fiction dreamed up by men who have nothing in their briefcases and a bad case of purse envy.

I love handbags even more than I do shoes – handbags always suit you, never make your legs look fat and sometimes you find money in them.

But you have to abide by a few bag lady rules:

• **Don't get too cute** Novelty handbags are fine for preteens and Japanese – but Hello Kitty does not work on a 36-year-old woman. Nor, incidentally, do hair clips, pigtails and capri pants.

• **Don't go out with a man who carries a handbag** Even platonically.

• **Don't give your handbags names** They are not babies or pets.

• **Avoid irony** 'Haven't we had that one already?' you're saying. That was shoes, pay attention, we're on to bags now, where the irony tends to be gilt and either swinging from or stuck to the offending item. Chains, unless from Chanel, should be used for snow tyres. Initials, unless they are your own and you're at prep school, should be worn with discretion – G on a buckle if you insist (you know the others) and LV printed on fabric if you are so insecure that you have to yell loadsamoney instead of carrying it around inside the purse, or if your lover is old, fat and ugly and you want everyone to think he is rich as well. And no fakes (we can tell). You don't want the biggest irony to be that you're the only person who doesn't get it.

Never, ever, ever buy one of those horrid things with custom pockets for calculators, pen holders or chequebook sleeves. You might be anal but you don't have to advertise it. Divisions, zip pockets and lots of compartments are fine – although you know you will never use them properly. If you really need to compartmentalise your life, have two basic handbags – one for playing, one for work. My handbag currently contains: a Cartier diary (blank) with accompanying pencil (blunt), a cocktail napkin from the Cipriani Hotel in Venice, seven boxes of matches, business cards (scattered across the bottom), a business-card holder, a mobile phone (battery flat), a notebook (but no pen), two menus, a Gucci wallet (empty), dark glasses, case for same, reading glasses (no case), a chequebook, a novel, a mirror, two lipsticks (red), YSL touche éclat and a toothbrush. And that's just for the evening. (I'm allowed to break my own rules.)

My work bag holds a credit card and another red lipstick, which brings me neatly to another of life's great pleasures.

Cosmetics – the sisterhood of slap Make-up is another fantasy purchase. I have more cosmetics than a troupe of drag artists. I have concealer, line filler, tinted moisturisers, eyebrow pencils, eye liner, mascara, eye shadows, blushers, powders and enough bottles of foundation to build a house on.

Of course it is all useless – and, frankly, ridiculous   given the raw material nature provided me with. In apartment terms I'm the fixer upper than no amount of paint will ever transform to Elle Decoration standards. We've all seen the woman perched at the beauty counter in a department store having her face made over and thought the words horse and bolted. Some of us have been that woman, getting the pitying glances from other customers who know that the blemishes spreading suburban sprawl across your cheeks are undisguisable. And then you have the ears to contend with.

Anyway, do you really want to let that girl with the fixed smile and the powder brush anywhere near you? She is not about to wave her applicator wand and grant your wishes – she's a nightmare. Do you realise that you risk coming out of the store wearing orange foundation and brown lip liner? Exactly.

These aren't make-up artists – they're still colouring in – that's why they need the lines around the eyes and the lips. There must be a rule in B-movie Beauty School that women who work on make-up counters have to look like a porn star's embalmed corpse. And that's before we even get to perfume girls. I love buying cosmetics, I just don't want to talk to anyone with the IQ of a cotton bud while I'm doing it. And admit it, when shopping for make-up – everyone's a cotton bud. There are three periods in life when an otherwise intelligent woman's brain turns to mush – when you're in lust, when you're pregnant and when you're in a store, buying cosmetics.

You have to send your intellect out for coffee and while it's away, pretend to believe in lipisomes and hydrience. You have to ask the girl with no brain for a natural blusher when you both know there is no such thing – unless you've tucked your knickers into your skirt. That's why it's always better to buy the stuff and take it home to play with.

Despite my conspicuous cosmetic consumption, I barely wear a thing. I used to try and disguise my freckles after a friend enthusiastically attempted to rub a particularly dark one from the side of my nose with a tissue. I would have been slightly more appreciative if she hadn't spat on it first. Make-up didn't work, I just looked as though I had been dead for a while. Freckles, to me, are what rosy cheeks are to other girls – they provide a bit of welcome colour to my face. I also tried a tinted moisturiser, not realising that it was also a fake tan which had the unhappy result of turning me into my own Mexican twin sister. Since then, I experiment carefully.

Occasionally I cover up dark circles under my eyes with ineffectual creams that act as the equivalent of neon signs flashing 'Look – bags!' whilst sniggering. The best known cosmetic for dark circles and eye bags is another of life's little desirables – a pair of sunglasses. The coverage is great, they come off and on, unlike mascara, without the need of paint stripper. They make you look sophisticated, glamorous and mysterious and conceal absolutely everything. Even a squint. Yes they also make you look exceptionally stupid if you're still wearing them when it's raining and you are at the cinema. So, either get a white stick, or move to a warm country and ski all winter. A further advantage of dark glasses is that you don't pierce people in the cheek with your mascara when you kiss them. I am a big fan of the sunglass treatment, but otherwise, I'm a bit of a natural non-beauty. It's either a brown paper bag with holes cut for the eyes, or a lick of lipstick and I'm all made up.

I like a tube of Nars Heatwave as much as the next vamp, but do I really think that it's going to make me infinitely desirable because it has nice black case and costs more than a bottle of vodka? Of course not – though a few shots of vodka actually does improve my face. All two of them. I know it's a only a thirty-something woman's youth separation anxiety, but I still adore the packaging, the advertising, the box, the bag and the bottle sitting happily ever after on my dressing table where I can admire it. I know I'm not getting a labrador puppy to cuddle like Liz Hurley just because I buy an eyeliner from Estée Lauder, but if I never have to sleep with Hugh Grant then I can live with it. However, I do want that little bit of glamour that you get with a voluptuous application of a brand new lipstick with a point as pert as a porn star's nipple, even if it's exactly the same shade as all my others. I like the sassy alligator snap of a new Chanel compact; the kiss of a sable brush sweeping across my face loaded with luminescent powder or the wet tip of an eyeliner licking my eyelids. Even better, every item comes at a fraction of the price of a new frock and you never cry in the changing room.

Any way you look at it, especially when drunk, back lit and without your glasses, make-up is a very good thing. There are so many ways that it changes your life for the better, not least of which is that you get to learn a foreign language – L'Oreal, Guerlain poudre visage et corps, Chanel poudre caresse avec pinceau applicateur, Decleor autobronzant lumiere... These days, every one's a linguist – by the time you've walked into the store, fronted up to the assistant and asked for some soin cosmetique solaire aux extraits de plantes, nipped next door to the coffee shop and ordered a grande latte, bought some take-away sashimi and visited Ikea for a course in Swedish DIY, the world is flat packed and lying in pieces at your feet, ready to assemble.

However, the law of make-up says that the older you get, the more you need, and the less you can get away with. Getting ready to go out is like packing for a vacation. You put it all in the suitcase and then take half of it back out. I do the same with make-up. I slap on the eye black and ladle on the foundation until I look like a one-woman Rocky Horror Show revival, and then I scrub it off again and make do with the bare minimum. I have to – I need the last half an hour to get into my hosiery.

Being in a tight embrace The most important things in my wardrobe are my tights. My mother told me that with the perfect legs you could hold a penny between your thighs, your knees, your calves and your ankles, and then – having a great pair of shapely pins herself – she would demonstrate. I felt deeply inadequate. I had long, thin legs that met so rarely, they had barely been introduced. I couldn't wear early tights because they didn't have elastic to hold themselves in and puckered unattractively around the knee. Furthermore they only came in two shades, American Tan and Rose Brown – i.e. Brazilian hooker and sunburn, neither of which suited Scottish, blinking in the sunlight, chicken legs.

Why a nation of women was raised to think American legs were the colour of choice I've no idea, but they made my life an early misery – well, that and the two knees waving at each other over the great divide.

But those happy days are gone – and so is the space in between. Now my legs meet all the way down and I could probably hold more pennies than a slot machine. My fantasies of barely there, silky stockings, long slim legs crossed at the knee and arching beguilingly are lost like the Easter Bunny once you have tooth decay. I often long in vain for the skinny legs of yesteryear – currently mine look as though they should be at the end of a pillar, holding up a building. So nowadays I buy black and put my faith in elastic and long skirts.

I always thank God when summer is over. No more bare legs, no more skimpy dresses and no more lumpy, Michelin-woman expanses of free flesh, pale and scared, between the bra and the knickers. I welcome autumn with my very own Harvest festival and instead of buying turkey on Thanksgiving, I buy tights – matte black, 60 denier, lycra, up-to-your armpits control-top tights. A man who once tried to smooth talk his way inside them described them as surgical tights – not realising a) that this isn't a chat-up line and b) in any case you need a lot of determination and metal cutters to get the things off. These babies are a fixture till spring, and then I pray for rain. Finally, it's safe to go back into the changing room. Suddenly, all my clothes fit and if I stop breathing I can almost look as though I have a flat, if somewhat expansive stomach. It's the rolling fields of middle England as opposed to the French Alps, but without the history and definitely no royal family.

Oooh, lovely, lovely tights – they're the modern answer to the corset and just as difficult to get on and off. Wearing them is like getting into a wetsuit, and if only they made them for the upper arms I'd die a happy, smoothed-out, lycra-constricted woman.

Talking Shop

How can anyone call shopping 'retail therapy'? For someone like me with the less-than-perfect figure, it feels more like aversion therapy. Taking your clothes off in a harshly lit, multi-mirrored communal changing room is a live performance of that dream where you find yourself walking down the street naked but here you don't wake up.

However, whenever my silhouette is seasonally squashed into submission I can be persuaded to rifle through the racks. Still, shopping is hell and curtained cubicles are the waiting room. Fashionistas may tell you that black is back – but for most of us it has never been away. It's camouflage, and the search for battle fatigues – the not-so little black dress – is an annual event. But you do have to do basic training.

First – toughen up Sadly having more subcutaneous fat than the shop assistant does not prevent you from feeling disenfranchised by shops that cater only for boys with breasts. Forget everything you read about the average woman being larger than a size 6. Lots of women are thin and gorgeous, almost all of them seem to work in shops and condescension is their weapon of choice.

Second – know your co-ordinates Sizes vary. On a scale of 1 to 4, four is jumbo and everything else is shopping in the children's department. American sizes run smaller than ours which must explain Gap's otherwise incomprehensible appeal. I mean, jeans, on me? Comeawn, honey – size 12 or no size 12, it's still like Montana on the move. European sizes are more troublesome. They are also fairly bewildering, as I found out recently when bulging unattractively in a seemingly shrink-to-fit black dress.

'What are you wearing and I'll see if have anything bigger,' screamed the shop assistant, like a sergeant major addressing the troops.

'Erm, it's a 42, sir,' I murmured, relieved it wasn't anything more incriminating like extra large. She turned to her colleague and raised her eyebrows. '14,' she hollered. They sighed in unison and pursed their purple lips ruefully. You know you've failed the physical.

Third – always do a reconnaissance of enemy territory Check there's a mirror in the changing room. Otherwise it means a walk across the sales floor, past a blonde stick insect smoothing a surgical bandage across her hip bones, towards your own fat reflection, enhanced – nay, illuminated – at the other end of the shop. If you're buttoned into a frock so tight that you look like a dog whose coat has shrunk, you don't need an audience. Beware also of trick mirrors – those that make you look thinner than you are. I know they are kind, but they are liars and other mirrors won't mind telling you the truth. After you've snipped the labels off and popped a few buttons.

And finally, watch your rear Though lycra tights are manna from large-hipped heaven, avoid anything else made of the same material. Some might say that lycra is the fat girl's friend, but to me it's the kind of friend who talks you into buying something that doesn't suit you just because it fits (and let's face it – lycra always fits), then laughs about you behind your back. Your large, dimpled back.

Just beat a retreat to base camp. After all – who really, really needs another not-so-little black dress to hang with the other thirty almost identical shrouds in the wardrobe? Go out and get a nice pair of black silk de luxe opaque tights instead. Everything will suddenly stand to attention.

Wake up, princess, it's back to reality

So far so gorgeous. In the words of that great philosopher and airport novelist Robert Parker: 'The more things you like the more opportunities you have to be happy.' So, okay – you like a lot of things and you deny yourself nothing. You're all set – you've booted yourself up, packed your bags and put on your war paint. You might even have sweated it out at the gym, lost weight, found the man of your dreams, had the baby you were desperate to pop before you were 35 and the career you've worked hard to achieve. So you're happy now – right?

Wrong. It doesn't work like that. Yes, lovely material things can put a little shine on an otherwise lacklustre life, but it's only polish. It chips, it fades, it goes out of fashion.

And although every woman may have a dominant Imelda Marcos gene, over-indulging it is another matter. Who can afford to take home every item they fall in love with? Eventually your wardrobe is littered with empty shoeboxes and designer shoe-bags all lying around like last week's lover's spare socks and toothbrush. I think that shopaholics like myself should initiate something along the lines of a lending library for shoes. After all, many times it's the thrill of the purchase that's the real pleasure. You just want to have the beautiful bag or the fuck-me-they're-high shoes in your possession for a little while. Eventually you ask, why? Is it worth it? Yes, you enjoy the flirtation, the excitement, the uncertainty – will I buy it, will it fit, will it suit me (who cares?) You love the little rush of the first moment that you slip your foot inside the virgin leather, the glory of the first date and the secret glances when you can't stop looking at them; the shiver of a silk scarf against the skin, or the little electric shock when that shoulder strap slides over your back for the first time. But you know the novelty won't last. Soon everything begins to pall, and feel familiar and boring. That's when you'd take it back, in pristine condition, to the shoe exchange and swop it for another to gloat over. Ah, if only you could do it with men too – except with my luck all the best ones would be out.

In the end a bag is a bag, and a shoe is just something to keep your feet dry. They are only objects to mark up and market and, just like men, they're all the same in the dark. Without a return and exchange policy, one day you ask yourself: Isn't it better just to stick with the one, solid item, love it, care for it and make a proper, long-term commitment?

No – that's what men are for. But they won't necessarily make you happy either. And who says you have to be happy, anyway?

Only a Presbyterian would think you're supposed to be miserable all the time, but it's only in fairy tales that the heroine lives happily ever after. In real life Cinderella would have been an abused child with a bad self-esteem problem and a long life of therapy stretching ahead of her, Sleeping Beauty would have been hospitalised, Snow White would have been arrested and Beauty would have been stuck with the Beast until divorce did them part. Life isn't fair and even though you try to combat your inner Calvinist, worshipping material goods won't do it either. The answer to most problems cannot be found in the shoe shop. Though you might try the bookstore.

Parallel parking your life – how to live vicariously

Spiritual salvation for me came in the form of Jilly Cooper, a writer of sex and shopping novels about posh people and their horses. I have never been on a horse in my life – and posh, to me, is merely the surprisingly common Spice Girl of the same name. But while I'd rather become a member of the Elvis Porcelain memorabilia club than read another book on How To Feng Shui my Bathroom Cabinet or Dance with my Cat, a trashy book is sometimes all you need to have a little rest from being yourself. Good old Jilly reminded me that a book can just be a story – it doesn't have to be earnest self-improvement or a tool to solve your problems. You can try on another life like a dress, but you don't have to hang it up afterwards. And if you join one of the reading groups which are proliferating worldwide since being popularised by auntie Oprah, you can get yourself a real live social life as well.

Almost everyone I know is in a reading group. In fact, almost everyone I know is in mine – and here's the thing: I love the group, but the reading has become more of a trial than a pleasure. It quickly became apparent that while I was quite happy to walk into a bookstore and leave with a copy of Oprah's book of the month, I hated having to talk about it afterwards. It was like having sex and then sitting down to a tutorial on technique. And you know, it's good to talk, but not in inverted commas, please.

It turned out that syntax doesn't really do it for me. While everyone else was discussing plot and characterisation, I couldn't get much beyond saying whether it was good for me or not. It seems I put my mind down somewhere in around 1985 and now can't remember where I left it. It must be in my other bag with my car keys.

Reading is one of the few totally absorbing activities you can do alone in bed, albeit with the lights on. It's the only solitary joy that can be discussed in polite society – the place where fantasy becomes reality and no one has to dress up in a maid's uniform or pretend to be Pedro the towel boy. A man I was madly in love with, until I discovered that his wife and two children shared the same feelings, once told me that he wished he had a parallel life so he could live it with me. It turned out that the parallel life was more of a parallel month of long lunches which earned him enough frequent flier miles on his credit card to go to Hong Kong and back – and me an extra seven pounds which I was mostly wearing on my hips. This is what they must mean by love handles.

But with a book you get the same kind of escape – the chance to be someone else for the space of 300 pages. You laugh, you cry, you get to sleep with the hero, but, happily, you don't have to eat the spaghetti and pretend to be his secretary when his friends walk in.

Reading a book is not childbirth – you don't necessarily want to go over it again and again – especially when all your friends have had C sections and, frankly, don't want to hear your superior stories of suffering. Nor are the study notes at the back of the book, especially designed for intelligent discourse, always encouraging. After reading a novel where I totally identified with the disillusioned, discontent heroine, I later read an interview with the author in which she confessed to finding her character a silly, selfish individual, whom she didn't really like.

Oh.

But I love all the sisterly solidarity in my book club, even though being with a whole bunch of women month after month brings with it a strong whiff of the school common room. First, you have to be good at verbal essays. Second, you have to wear your coolest clothes. Third, and most importantly, there are always alliances which you feel shut out of like an awkward schoolgirl. There is the Head Girl who everyone adores and wants to sit next to in class, there is the Swot who knows everything and loves telling you her grades, and the ambitious one who always wants to be first. I mostly just gaze at the clock and long for recess.

I have a keener interest in the soap opera of our lives than in the literary merit of our reading material. I know I am not pulling my intellectual weight and sometimes I make excuses like an adulterous lover for missing our meetings, and often skim just the first and last chapters so I can pretend to have read the book. I don't love the group for its mind – it's the body-talk I really, really want. Because after we've finished squeezing the joy out of every novel I have ever hoped to enjoy, we finally get down to gossip. Forget Proust and tell me about your Pilates instructor, wax lyrically about smooth legs and recite the names of all your sexual partners. Furthermore, twists in the plot often mirror real life and elicit a whole string of juicy My True Stories, all much stranger than fiction. Confession comes easier when Madame Bovary has done it all first.

My friend Julia says it's Tupperware party meets literary salon – an excuse to get together and bond, but without the need to buy a cereal container with snap-tight lid. But a word to those who have not embraced Catholicism and feel the need to seriously

unburden themselves. Think Tupperware and remember that
therapist. If you're already paying for a woman to do your hair
and another to file your nails – go the whole hog, pay someone
to listen to your neuroses and snap your lips shut in an air-tight
seal. You will feel so much better not having suddenly blurted out
an Evangelical affection for the female baby-sitter after a frank
discussion of *Oranges Are Not the Only Fruit*. Believe me, they
might be smiling benignly, but they're talking about you in the
bathroom afterwards.

And if you can't face the shrink, then get yourself another kind
of book, and write it all down.

The stationery life – or how to manage your Filofax fetish

Please tell me I'm not the only one with a fetish for stationery.
Well, deny it if you will – I know I'm not. I recently went out to
dinner with a hoary old hack who chain-smokes Marlboro and
confessed to a hard core S&M habit before we had even opened
the wine. As I was planning on reviewing the restaurant I got out
my trusty notebook and began to take notes along the lines of:
'Bloody hell, how will I survive three hours of this?' But the minute
he saw my PVC notebook, he had it out of my hands and began
stroking it as though it was a Persian cat.

'Ooooh, lovely paper, what weight would you say it was?' he
purred, fingering the leaves. 'And a fantastic kinky cover, where
did you get it?' As he spoke he twanged the elastic page retainer
as though it was a suspender attached to a sheer black stocking.
And since I'd shown him mine, he immediately showed me his –
a leather-bound book with hand-stitched vellum and marbled
endpapers. Not a very impressive size, but small and perfectly
formed. I gasped in appreciation.

'Do you want to hold it?' he urged, sounding not unlike the
kind of man you warn your children against. This led the
conversation away from in-house dungeons and on to the safer
topic of our shared obsession – watermarks and paper quality. He

was much more of a connoisseur than I and claimed to have shelves and shelves of beautifully bound notebooks. Though, in retrospect, as a chat up line his 'Feel my hand-tooled leathers' might have meant anything.

As in all things, I'm little more than a profligate. I'm constantly out looking for Mr Good Book and cannot walk past a stationers without walking in and buying something to write in. I have the United Nations of Notebooks, in all sizes, shapes and colours – the classic, the ethnic, the old-fashioned and the trendy. I have them with spiral binding and held together with artfully tied string, I have them with designer logos and royal warrants and I have them covered in Chinese silk with pages made from what looks like pre-World War I toilet paper. They share only one thing in common – that they are all mostly empty.

I mean, I want to write in them, it's just so difficult to bring myself actually to defile all that pristine white space with my scribbled handwriting. Of course, I promise myself that I'll keep it neat and stylish, and often start off well – setting out the first couple of pages like a graphic design project, but sooner or later, I get embarrassingly sloppy. Put it this way, I don't want to get knocked down and have the nurse flicking through these babies trying to identify me – she's more likely to send me for a Psych consult.

To me, each notebook is like the first day of the rest of my life, the beginning of a diet, the vow to behave myself in public, to swear always to remove my make-up before I sleep instead of topping it up the next morning, and to drink more water. It's the beginning of a new organised system of restaurant notation where I never doodle or play hangman, and always write in copperplate. It's the new novel I haven't written or the posthumously published diary, complete with illustrations – something along the lines of *Country Diary of an Edwardian Lady* but without the wild flowers.

Somehow, an outline sketch of my hand, a series of anonymous phone numbers, the odd lipstick blot and 'fish not very fresh' written in the handwriting of an autistic after three vodka martinis, doesn't look very publishable. It's not even *Bridget Jones's*

Diary – at least she managed faithfully to record her weight, cigarettes and alcohol intake. Even if I could remember mine, I know I would only lie.

Keeping a journal is a wonderful thing, but the first rule of a diary should always be to maintain truth and privacy. This is fine for the fictional Ms Jones who could fearlessly record the minutiae of her sex life. But she lived alone. Family life and trust are like safe and sex – they should go together but then – hey – if we're talking shoulds here then I'm an Italian Principessa and only look overweight. Think back – as a teenager, how many of your mothers found out about the secret drunken parties and the loss of your virginity by 'accidentally' reading your diary? This is why she gives you one as a present, age about eight, with an ineffectual gold key the size of an ant, and a lock you can open with a paperclip. It's so she can start reading your diary just about the time when she stops being able to read your mind. Do you think your kids or your partner are any less given to temptation? If you live by yourself, get rid of your angst between the sheets of an A5 notebook. If you live with interested parties, think of a great hiding place where no one ever looks. In my case somewhere between my chin and my knees would be about right.

At home, my family's idea of respecting privacy is to yell out before opening the bathroom door. Leaving a dairy anywhere visible would be like taking out an ad in the newspaper saying 'Read Me'. Especially now that I have a teenage daughter of my own.

As a result, whenever I start trying to keep an honest diary I immediately get paranoid and afraid to write anything of consequence. What's left is hardly the stuff of posterity – I mean, do you care if it was raining on July 20 1997? Big deal – in Britain, it's always bloody raining. I have tried code, but that doesn't work either. Who can remember a person's name five years after the event, let alone what the lines, squiggles and oblique references to 'washed my hair three times' were supposed to mean?

So my truth is all a fiction, and my fiction is hyperbole. Just as a novelist is God of the world he or she creates, so have I been known to get a little creative in mine. If anyone reads the few journals I have managed to write after my death, I'm damned if they are going to think I'm a dull, middle-aged woman with cellulite and the sex life of a giant panda. In a journal written during a trip to New York in 1980, I'm amused to read that I had a fantastic time full of Manhattan night clubs and sight-seeing when, as I remember it, I spent a lot of time crying in a studio apartment in Brooklyn. And I seem to have been only about sixteen at the time.

So I'm not a reliable diarist. I can hardly keep a date book going. But I still buy gold-tipped agendas and five-year journals, as though I was Samuela Pepys, and continue to write my notes on the back of old envelopes. However, every time I start a new commission or writing job, I go out and buy a new notebook which I do use. This is because I get superstitious. If the article never gets published, or the job gets cancelled, then the notebook especially bought for the purpose is relegated to the unclean, unlucky shelf tainted with the whiff of failure, and is never opened again. These books are like cheating lovers. You can't ever trust them again.

The lovely, brand new, blank ones – now they still have endless possibilities which make me very, very happy.

The car – driving yourself to distraction

But if you're keeping the faith, the journal and a regular appointment with the shrink, and your bank balance is diminishing but not your problems, it's worth considering the advice of psychotherapist Dorothy Rowe, who claims that two fundamental tools for beating depression are a job with a salary, and a car. She's right about the car – it's another thing that offers endless possibilities for recreational pleasure and, by default, happiness. The freedom you get from a car really does help to beat depression – well, until you get the garage bills. For those of you

who live in car-dominated societies where life without one seems impossible, have pity on your sisters who always take the bus. It does happen. Because I am married to a man who doesn't drive – yes, such peculiar creatures do exist – for years I was the irritating woman on public transport with two kids under three, a double pushchair and six bags of shopping. However, once I had learned to drive, a whole new world unravelled before me: happy hours on the highway in a Peugeot 205 with two children under five strapped in the back listening to 'The Wheels on the Bus', with a screaming infant lodged in a baby seat in the front, while I drove with one hand and held a bottle with the other. It was even more tricky while I was still breast-feeding. But I was very popular with other drivers.

A car is independence. It's that 'Ballad of Lucy Jordan' cliché of driving around with the wind in your hair. It makes you feel totally in control and yet still spontaneous. After years of being married to husband number 1, who regularly punctuated our arguments with a slamming door and the jingling of his car keys, it was liberating to be able to do the same myself. Though coming back to borrow money for petrol doesn't do much for your exit technique.

To a man, a car is supposedly both an expression of his virility, or lack thereof, and an extension of his office. Think about it – put a bloke inside his motor and suddenly he's a gay man. Everything is neat and tidy – the jacket hung on a little peg in the back, when at home he slings it on the back of a chair. The leather upholstery is squeaky clean, the surfaces uncluttered, he uses air freshener and turtle wax. He has his mobile phone, his laptop in his little briefcase on the passenger seat, and a dashboard blinking with gadgets such as a satellite guidance system, where a woman's voice tells him how to get from A to B in much the same way as a road map – except you can't yell at a road map (which explains why the voice is female – it stands in for the wife). Then there is the name plate on the office door – DARREN written across the windscreen, or a set of vanity plates saying PEN 1S. This is before we even get to the executive toys such as little steel balls dangling from the rear view mirror. Hmm, and they think we're insecure.

Men are preoccupied with engine size, bodywork and the technical specifications of the particular model. But to many a woman, a car is just a handbag on wheels – big enough to lug around half the contents of the supermarket, your own kids and their visitors, several pairs of shoes and a full range of cosmetics – though I warn you, from experience, that lipstick does have a tendency to melt when the car gets hot. A car is a microscopic, self-propelling world in which you can sing along with your own choice of music, fornicate and eat potato chips – though preferably not all at the same time. The huge drawback however is that while in a handbag your mess is concealed, a car has windows.

A shame, that. Tinted windows are a boon to the modern woman. Not to mention the modern man. His car may well be tidy, but I could die happily without ever seeing another man pick his nose in a traffic jam.

Where I grew up only men could drive. This was back in the unreconstructed days when men were men and women were passengers. They seemed to have been born with a microchip implanted in their thighs which only allowed them to navigate, so naturally I wanted a sex change. My dad had a four-door family saloon, my brother a beaten-up Ford Escort with tigerprint seat covers and I had a sedate thick-wheeled Raleigh bicycle which I pretended was a pony named Turk, and stabled every night in the garden shed after gently covering it with a blanket.

So my mother couldn't teach me much about driving, except how to wear a headscarf and sit smoking cigarettes in the passenger seat. My father loved to go out in the car, but hated to stop anywhere. The idea was to go for a scenic drive and return three hours later without ever having left the car. Thankfully, I left the Land Before Time and discovered that you don't need a Y chromosome to drive a car, and – wonders – you needn't look wistfully at blurred beauty spots and public restrooms on the highway, but you can stop and get out.

Furthermore, because husband number 2 doesn't drive, he gets to do all the map reading. In effect this merely means that we always leave dinner parties half an hour early to allow us to get lost and have the obligatory argument in the car on the way home, but it's a nice idea in theory. Currently my babemobile is a seven-seater space wagon with a CD player stocked with sing-along songs. Believe me – once you have kids you leave the charts behind and enter the realm of Compilation Tapes – if you know the words to all the songs of Elvis Presley's greatest hits and Burt Bacharach, you can drown out the noise of their incessant whining as they ask, 'Are we there yet?' But I do still dream of convertible sports cars and secretly long for a chance to practise being a dick for the day.

A flashy, fast car dawdling at the traffic lights gets a Pavlovian response from almost any man. In Roman times, men used to wear little gold scale models of their dangly bits strung around their necks to increase their machismo; these days, you get yourself a sports car. Preferably a red one. As a woman, I'm not immune to the charms of a machine that accelerates fast enough to flatten me, and anything else requiring support, against the back of my seat. It acts like a mini face-lift with extra cleavage. And if there's no room for the weekly supermarket shop – so much the better.

However, my one shot at bringing out my inner wanker was

somewhat spoiled when I managed to trap myself in a borrowed, low-slung Lotus Elise at a car park exit where I'd stopped too far away from the ticket machine to reach it, and too close to open the door. I sat there for what seemed like five years until I eventually managed to hail a passing employee to rescue me. There are times when being a woman is a mercy. Your testosterone tends to trickle down the exhaust pipe when you're trapped impotently behind a ticket barrier.

If I'm honest, my husband's lack of driving ability makes me very susceptible to a passing man who can change gears and the radio station while still keeping his hand on your knee. But on the other hand, the free one, since he can't drive, it means I get the car all to myself. A real power trip.

The job – working through your problems

There is no doubt that work can be one of the most rewarding aspects of life. However, I've done enough low-level, low-paid menial jobs to understand that it's not all power breakfasts and conference calls. I've done the photocopying, I've bought the sandwiches. I've even made the sandwiches.

Nevertheless, in my working life, I have been incredibly lucky. I haven't scaled the dizzying heights of material or corporate success. I don't own an attaché case, a business suit, or run a company car – and unless there's a multinational crying out for women who can ask for coffee in six languages, make a Batman costume from a pair of tights and an apron, and simultaneously cook, help with homework, listen to a recorder practice and worry about copy deadlines, I have no transferable skills. But I do what I can, I love what I do, am able to devote as much or as little time as I like to it – and occasionally people pay me for it.

When I was at home with my children I was a woman with many accomplishments but no purpose beyond that of getting through the day without committing infanticide. I felt deeply inferior to my working friends who had jobs, lives outside the home, money in the bank and luncheon vouchers, while I felt like a domestic appliance with very low running costs. Hell, my lunch was spooning pap into a child from a safe distance so I didn't have to wear it for the rest of the day. As a result I overcompensated, trying to excel at everything within my sphere just to prove how efficient I was. I was Supermum – I made forts from cereal boxes and a whole set of hand-painted roller blinds. I volunteered with an adult literacy scheme, studied Arabic in the evenings and became a moving blur of DIY, faux paint finishes, home-made play-doh, gourmet dinners and endless part-time jobs undertaken in my spare time – that is, at an hour when any normal person would have been asleep. I was a part-time everything and a full-time mess. It wasn't until another friend told me that she could just picture me living in the country keeping hens that I realised there were limits to my home-making aspirations. Though livestock did have a certain appeal – when you get fed up with chickens you can cut their heads off and cook them. Children you can only put to bed. After a story.

But didn't you ever have a proper job? Haven't you worked? asked a career-driven female recently, as though I had three heads and had not thought of lopping the other two off.

To women like this, work – and probably sex – are only legitimate if you get paid for them. Full-time childcare is seen as an occupation fit only for brain-dead housewives. The only way a woman can look after children and still be socially acceptable is if she's their nanny. This disapproving, She Ra jet-setter has several children – two in boarding school and a baby looked after by a full-time nanny. She has her own issues and insecurities, not least of which is that, although she's on the top step of corporate life, she also weighs 300 pounds and her relationship with her children is conducted mostly through the telephone.

No one has it easy. But it would be less difficult if women didn't stick it to each other because of the personal choices they've made. Furthermore, not all women have those choices –

some have to work to pay the mortgage and some who would like to work in full-time employment can't earn enough to pay the full-time childcare.

Thanks to a short spell being barking mad in suburbia, and several years staring at the ceiling in a shrink's office, my manic Martha Stewart period ended with a bang and a lot of whimpering. I gave up trying to prove my own worth with wallpaper and embraced inadequacy instead. I threw in the tea towel, hung up my marbling brush, chucked in the dreary evening school essays and the dismal part-time jobs, and went to art college. Sloth became my new busy. I sat down and stopped feeling guilty.

Success on its own might give you a warm glow when you stop to reapply your lipstick in the executive washroom as you make your way up the corporate ladder, but too many of us equate busy-ness and achievement with fulfilment. 'I have a busy life,' they say proudly as though it was a positive character trait, when really they are running around like self important whirling dervishes, wearing stress, the proud accessory of success, pinned like a brooch to the lapel of their well-cut Jill Sander suit.

These days women can do whatever they want. If they want to be queen of the corporate world, Prime Minister or Chief Justice they can do it. If you want it, go for it, but don't kid yourself that there's no trade-off – and don't come whining when there's something in life's toy shop that you can't have. Until they clone you, it's impossible to be everywhere and do everything. You don't get extra credit in heaven for being an over-achiever. Once you're dead, no one is going to remark on how effective you were in the office. Once you are buried in the sod, even if you get a big fat obituary in *The Times* with an air-brushed, much-younger picture, no one except your nearest and dearest are going to remark much on you at all. So, enough already. Do something you enjoy and which empowers you – if you're good at it, if you excel at it, if you make a difference and it inspires, comforts or sustains you, so much the better. If it doesn't – then find a passion outside work that does. Though fancying Ben Affleck doesn't count.

Success is having a job that fulfils you. Happiness, however, is having your *own* money. If the two come together, give yourself a round of applause. If you're happy carving busts of the Iron Maiden from soap, have enough down time to spend with your loved ones, and you can support yourself, you're a success. We all know that money doesn't make you happy, but not having any at all really sucks.

I firmly believe that you can have it all – you just can't have it all at the same time – you have to take it in instalments and make three or four easy payments to yourself. And there are penalties you can't avoid. However even with a bank balance to boast of, a fantastic, creative job, two homes, a yacht and a holiday in St Barts twice a year, if you're still miserable – then you're probably either suffering for terminal discontentment or you're looking for someone to love you who doesn't charge by the hour.

Getting some class...

Or maybe you're dissatisfied because you just fancy a change? I might as well tell you now that practically anything you do throughout the first half of your working life, you will invariably not want to continue doing during the second. You're an architect but you want to study law. You're a lawyer who wants to retire early and keep pot-bellied pigs. You're a painter who wants to be an accountant. You're a wife who wants a divorce. You're a menopausal mistress who wants a baby. Midlife crisis, sabbatical, adventure, nervous breakdown, self-realisation or pottery – call it what you will. but suddenly you want to start over. So you need tools. Look no further than adult education.

First – get the manual At the start of every semester I used to dance through the listings of available subjects as though it was a box of chocolates, thinking, mmm – shall I go for the soft centres this year – Art Nouveau Cake Decoration or maybe Elementary Line Dancing? Or will I choose one of the hard, difficult to chew subjects like Economics? Speed is essential. You have to enrol quickly or all the best ones are gone. Then you'll be left with Intermediate French and end up spitting it out halfway through the term when it becomes obvious that while you're struggling to remember your grade school declensions, everyone else has a summer house in Burgundy and is merely swaggering like a Francophile bodybuilder on muscle beach.

Second – polish your nails – I mean skills Being a mature student – i.e. over college admission age – is nothing to be ashamed of. Or so the prospectuses claim. But frankly, there's nothing mature about stumbling over the present tense of etre at the age of 41. It's the shame of being the only pupil in Kindergarten who can't tie her own shoelaces revisited. Except this time mummy doesn't settle you in at your desk, and you aim to get through the class without having an accident and leaving wearing the spare knickers.

So pick something palatable. Otherwise you risk post-Christmas burn-out when, traditionally, everyone is fed up with the dark, cold nights and *The Sopranos* seems a better option than carving decoy ducks in the local high school. Because I left school unfashionably early with extra credit for an inferiority complex of superior dimensions, I've had plenty of practice at skills honing. I did extra A levels during my first job in a strange city, a part-time evening-based degree in my late twenties when I had two children and a crushing desire to prove I could do more than lego construction. Then I dabbled: linguistics, computers – as one does – and years and years of cooking school which somehow is more fun in a test kitchen than in my own. This was followed by the after dinner mints of all courses – the most protracted Art and Design degree known to middle aged woman, which I did as a midlife-crisis-torn mother of four.

It certainly was an education – a long exercise in how to feel small when you're very, very large. Imagine being the oldest student by almost fifteen years. Imagine being older than even your teachers, having more kids than the rest of the class combined and the only woman with the mercilessly conventional thing known as Husband. Imagine being at art school and discovering that you can't actually tell the difference between magenta and magnolia – unless they are children in your kid's class at school. Then factor in that I wasn't studying marriage guidance or law with the other grown-up, retired and downsized housewives. I had enrolled at a temple of scruffy youthdom, planning to spend my days piddling about with paint. I was going to sit around in a studio talking about post-modernism when I already felt so post, post-modern as to be thoroughly past it.

Communicate your needs, assemble friends and lubricate well

On day one you think, who will talk to me? Who will sit next to me in the cafeteria? You've got the new bag, the pristine set of new sketchbooks in more sizes than the Marks & Spencer's bra department, the jumbo Pritt stick, the fistful of sharpened pencils and a whole spectrum of fat tubes of paint. However, these only serve to make you even more conscious of your conventional, overly mature status. No one else had even thought to bring paper. Who needs pencils? Figurative drawing is dead, and conceptual art is not a new method of birth control.

My fellow students smoked dubiously perfumed roll-ups while my only bad habit was a packed lunch in a floral plastic box and coffee in a vacuum flask. No one else did the coursework because they were all – like, man, sooo busy raving/sleeping/having sex. I was Mrs Boring Goodie Two Shoes and did everything on time. I didn't have a life, I just had a family. I was as hip as a macramé potholder and only half as useful.

But eventually I adapted. I squeezed myself into jeans and forced myself not to iron them. I made a couple of friends – usually those with mental health problems. As anyone who does evening classes will know, adult education is the equivalent of nursery school for those in care in the community. Art for the lonely, the lost and the just plain loopy. But you need allies – mine was a hirsute vegetarian, who practised astral healing and didn't drink alcohol or eat processed food. Actually, she didn't seem to eat any food. She would watch me munch my way through a bag of cheese and onion potato chips as though expecting me to find Satan nesting at the bottom of the packet rather than a promotional scratch card. She wouldn't fill her body up with a whole lot of chemicals, she said. Ooh no – not unless they had mind-altering qualities and kept you up all night.

Hey – for that I had children.

Admire your handiwork I can't say I grew in confidence, but I did grow a very thick skin. Standing in front of 50 people listening to your work being publicly deconstructed by a baby-faced balding bloke in dungarees at a Friday afternoon crit was a living nightmare. Grown men cried and he wasn't even talking about them.

But happily, after that – nuclear war, loan refusals, falling stock – pfuh, water off a decoy duck's back. Suddenly, anything – well, except intermediate French – seemed possible. Life can start again. Phase 2 – the sequel.

On Being Faithful

Having religious faith can be a great comfort to many people. But the problem with monotheistic religions is that it sure as heck puts a lot of strain on the supreme deity to be all things to all women. It's like expecting to find a life partner who is a company director, a do-it-all handyman, a hands-on father, a national sports champion and good looking.

If you find this man there is going to be a queue longer than the one waiting for the Ladies Room at a Tom Jones concert. So the way I look at it, if you say little prayer to God – Chuck – the big guy has better things to do than find you a space to leave your car less than a day's forced march away from the supermarket. Surely he delegates? I imagine that the heavenly hierarchy is sort of like the Police: There's the Chief – the important man – looking after law and order, and a whole subsection of meter maids, who take care of parking violations, with speed cameras for the really unimportant stuff.

So whatever it is you put your faith in, never discount the lesser known deities – the celestial photocopiers, the sandwich makers and the ones who help you navigate through life and park in the street of your choice.

Use them or lose them – it's surely only a matter of time before they're automated. *Thank you for calling heaven. Your prayer is held in a queue. If your prayer is love related, please press 1. If it is related to money, illness or love, please wait for an operator. Your call will be answered as soon as someone is available to take your prayer. However, if you have a touch tone phone, please listen to the following options:*

Press 1 for the God of Parking Life is not all easy riding – especially if you live in an over-populated city. You can drive around in the car but you can't get out because you can't bloody park it. Whenever I'm circling the block for the seventh time, looking in vain for somewhere within three miles of the store I want to visit I say a little prayer to the God of Parking.

She's out there looking after you – but just like Tinkerbell, she only exists if you believe in her. Nor is she always totally reliable. For a start she has her favourites: the privileged – who she can do nothing about, but hey – if their name is stencilled on the wall, then the space stays empty until they get there; and men (who are usually the same as the privileged). It's got to be true – I can see no other reason why it's always a bloke in a Mercedes the size he wishes his willy was, who takes up two clearly demarcated spaces seconds before I get there.

But like most females she is open to persuasion. A few, please, please, pleases, a pressing need to visit the loo, and the threat of tears (all women are suckers for blubbering, unless the perpetrator is under five – when you learn to screen) can often suffice to open up a gap in the parking garage like Moses parting the Red Sea. But Moses was lucky – he didn't have to reverse.

Now, I can reverse. I just can't do it in public. Whenever I have to reverse in full view of an audience, I suffer from performance anxiety and just cannot get it in. So I sweat, I curse, I whimper, and if I'm really stuck I get my husband to wave me in with the self-importance of General Schwartzkoff directing the troops in Desert Storm. All in all, it's a very deflating experience.

In these circumstances, the God of Parking isn't much help. She probably can't do reverse either.

Press 2 for Saint Nicotine Saint Nicotine is a fallen Angel – a deadly, no-good, dirty low-down demon who, if you don't have the brain of a particularly stupid gerbil and listened to your mother, you'll have given a wide berth and refused to join his carcinogenic cult.

Unfortunately, my mother was a disciple.

Saint Nicotine and I had an on-and-off-again relationship for years – something akin to having a sordid, illicit affair with an old lover that you just can't break. It was a craving that I thought had been dead for fifteen years but, just like flares, it keeps coming back – and after one reckless act at a party, I turned from a born again non-smoker into a ash-anointed follower of old Saint Nic.

It's a filthy habit, but Joe Smoke takes away your sense of smell and surrounds you with other deluded disciples. No longer are you standing at parties looking as useful and as decorative as an aspidistra, anxiously clutching a drink as if it was the only thing between you and the last lifeboat on the Titanic; instead you're basking in the devoted company of other smoke-heads and enjoying – while you can still breathe – the ready camaraderie that exists between anyone sharing a soft pack.

In all affairs, your partner is always the last to know. Like any other cheating wife I began spending hours washing away the evidence in the bathroom. I took to carrying my own airline-size toothpaste and toothbrush in my purse. I ate Tic Tacs and took a lot of walks with our non-existent dog. From being a evangelical anti-tobacco campaigner who banned smokers from even striking a match inside the house, I became a duplicitous, chain-smoking hypocrite.

They say time is a great healer, but my

wheezing heart still contracts with the lovesick agony of a teenager whenever I run into Marlboro man and I passively smoke with the mindless ardour of a pre-teen on a Britney Spears tour. A friend told me that he thinks about football fixtures and goal averages whenever he's trying to maintain an erection; oooh very romantic – Aston Villa 1 Norwich City 2 – yeah baby. I have employed the same tactics to take my mind off cigarettes and all I can say is, if he has the same results as me, I don't think his women can be very satisfied.

So we are all agreed on this – stay away from Saint Nicotine and do not turn to him in moments of stress. Since I'm not your mother, I'll leave the warnings to the Surgeon General. Apart from a range of debilitating and fatal illnesses, let me be blunt – while waiting to shuffle off to that great big ashtray in the sky, your clothes and hair will stink like a bar-room floor and no one will kiss you, except other smokers who are a very bad insurance risk.

Also you spend way too much time standing shivering outside public buildings.

Press 3 for the Patron Saint of Afternoon Television For shut-ins everywhere there's a whole cast of saviours in the form of magazine chat-show hosts and wooden actors with full make-up, big hair and shoulder pads – and that's just the men. You might have no friends and your life might bite, but at least you don't live in a world of shifting scenery, meaningful pauses and very bad dialogue.

Yes it's mindless, but that's the point. It's a reassuring place to be: plump women get paid for sitting on a sofa all day chatting, while over in soap-opera land, anything is possible. Problems are resolved in the space of three episodes, characters die and are either forgotten by the time the titles roll, or come back next week in a different-coloured wig, resurrected as their long-lost twin sister. Children, helpfully, go overseas or interstate, never to be seen again – unless they transmogrify into a different body – and when there's a marriage, they only have to invite the members of the cast, because these people really don't have any friends. Even better, in soap-opera land, once your siblings have been written out of the series you needn't ask them to your wedding, or if they come, you don't have to talk to them – they are, mysteriously, always off camera. But you do get to see once-upon-a-big-time Hollywood actresses who can't get a role on stage in a British theatre, suddenly appear in cameo guest spots.

The Patron Saint of Afternoon Television offers you a continuity sadly lacking in modern life. Husbands may come and go, children grow up and leave home, but Falconcrest goes on and on for ever, showing on a loop on a cable station somewhere near your sofa. As a big-time soap addict I've known the cast of some longer than most of my friends. I don't know my neighbours but I do know every single person in *Dallas*. And like old friends, you run into some of them over and over again – catching them later in *Melrose Place* and *Spin City*.

You can see people with trashy lives socking each other senseless on bare-it-all confessional couches, and you can see people with empty lives on *Survivor* and *Big Brother*, locked up on an island or in an isolated house, publicly hating each other.

These programmes would be ideal vehicles for public figures and world leaders. You could send off Sinn Fein, Tony Blair and Ian Paisley and settle the Irish Question; George Bush and Saddam Hussein for the Gulf War; or the Whole Cast of the Middle East Conflict and just leave them to vote each other out. The viewers at home, after watching them plot, scheme, eat grubs and fail to do the washing up, could decide who eventually wins – and finally we would all have world peace.

If religion is the opium of the masses then Afternoon TV is two aspirins and a cup of cocoa – a legal anaesthetic that dulls the mind and soothes the spirit. It's always there for you. You may not take comfort in it every day, or even every year, but you know that you can always switch on, switch off and find comfort in cardboard people.

Press 4 for the God of Computer Solitaire As pointless gods go, this is the spoutless teapot. However there are those who set good store by him. Work cannot begin until a few choruses of the Klondike have been sung, and many a phone call is punctuated with the steady click, click, click of Patience playing out in the background. It's like saying your rosary – three games of Freecell and one of Aces High. Computer software designers understand this and thoughtfully provide a number of irritatingly addictive games on every home PC.

As a meditative practice, you're better off counting your paperclips, as Computer Solitaire freezes you up as effectively as keeping your knickers in the ice box. There is no room for either logical thought or lateral thinking – your entire brain is concerned with whether you can find a space to put your King of Hearts. Nevertheless, there are those who attach a great mystical significance to getting all the cards on top of the aces. It's like the I Ching of time-wasting. You think about your problem and then promise yourself that if you can just get the next game to work out then everything will be fine and you'll finally get down to work. Then it's best of three. Then it's one in ten. Then it's lunch.

But it's a false God. The guy you met in the bar the night before will not ring just because you finally win a game of Chinese Patience. You will not get the job you applied for because you managed to finish a game of Freecell. I know. Otherwise, in return for the 3,692 games I've played of the bugger, I'd have won Columnist of the Year.

I know, because after a particularly stressful intervention, I had to have three kinds of Patience and a variation on the theme of Mah-jong forcibly removed from my computer so that I could start work before 11.30 every morning. It's like being in a cult – you need rescuing from yourself.

Press 5 for the God of Lost Socks This is another unreliable deity whom many of us nevertheless consult on a daily basis. Not only is she responsible for odd socks but she has a particular interest in single gloves, assorted jewellery – particularly rings – keys, credit cards and the fiver you had in your hand a minute ago. I think she also has my mind somewhere about her person which no amount of pleading will make her give back.

You can have her on automatic redial and ring back – sometimes she listens and sometimes, just like your mother, to teach you a lesson she refuses to respond. It would be much better if you just remembered where you put things, paired your socks before throwing them in the laundry, hung up your car keys on the hook you fixed especially for the purpose and always put your money and cards safely back inside your purse.

Except for the gloves – why do you think they come with little strings on the end? Gloves, umbrellas and your youth are made to get lost. You might as well get used to it.

Friendship

Ah. friends. Can't live with them, can't live without them – well, you can, but then you have no one to shop with, to watch weepy films with or to moan to about men. My mother was always much more successful at friendship than I was, given that I seemed to spend half the time sulking with my childhood friends and the other half feeling aggrieved. Her only advice when I complained that I had no one to play with was 'Och, never mind, hen' – 'hen' being the quaint endearment employed by Scottish mothers who think calling your child after poultry is a token of love. This advice came back to me recently when a friend admitted she was very depressed and unhappy, and had gone into therapy. So, what's the problem, I asked. 'I just really want everyone to like me,' she replied. God, so that's a problem? I thought it was just human nature.

I came to terms with the fact that I was never going to win any popularity contests ('never mind' is actually fairly good advice), but I'm definitely feeling a little queer these days. After years of bonding with the disenfranchised fat, simple, spotty girls at school after it became obvious I was never going to be Prom Queen, when I finally made a good friend, I married him – and we've been joined at the hip of holy matrimony longer than anyone else I know. So you might think that I'd be feeling deprived and that my heart would be pitter-pattering in desperation at the sight of Brad Pitt with his kit off, or Pierce Brosnan with his gun in his hand, but it just isn't happening. Instead of lusting after unattainable men with impossible bodies, I've started to fancy girls.

The friend on a pedestal with really great shoes Straight women can put their handbags down and stop looking so worried – they are quite safe. I am not a lipstick lesbian. Nor have I developed a sudden longing for a sapphic one-night stand just to make sure I dropped my glove for the right gender. I mean – sisterly snogging, it's not like Venice, you don't really have to do it once before you die. It's not that I have anything against women – after all I am one – but when it comes to breasts, I want mine to be the only pair being bared.

No, fancying women is more like hero worship. Just a little crush or three – a case of serial sorority. You get to a certain age and the world suddenly seems to be full of successful, funny, intelligent, beautiful women and you want to experience what it's like to have all of them. Or at least sit next to them in class and be their new, very, very best friend.

In my group of friends – which admittedly, given our self-styled name, the bitches' club – does not immediately conjure up 'warm and cuddly' – women-fancying is alive and well and causing just as much rivalry as men-fancying ever could. The reason is Susan – who is slim, gorgeous and staggeringly clever and the object of almost everyone's affections. We all want to bask in her friendly, supportive, good-humoured glow, and vie with each other to be the most favoured friend, falling over ourselves to offer her lifts to and from the furthest reaches of Suburbia – even when we live in the opposite direction. Sadly, just like men, you know when they're not interested. She's obviously a lot keener on Isobel than on anyone else, though I can't see what the big attraction is. Isobel can't even drive.

And with women, there's no point in unveiling your cleavage or fluttering your eye-lashes – sex isn't a weapon in the battle for popularity. You've just got to face it – you are the one who kisses up. Not the one who holds the cheek.

This is something of a trend for me – I always fancy the unattainable ones. My first was a middle-class neighbour with cut-glass vowels and a boarding-school background. Just the sight of her wholesome, golden-girl looks as she loped down the road, a labrador in each hand and a gaggle of tow-headed children clinging on to her green wellies would make my heart leap like a salmon. I'd watch her, adrift amongst the sea of Gucci-scarved mothers in the playground, and listen entranced to her recipes for woodcock and pheasant – the things that woman could do with a small bird and a tub of double cream were legendary. She was a Goddess of housekeeping. She made gravy without granules, exercised her boys as if they were dogs twice a day in the park, and ran an art gallery in her spare time. She threw impromptu dinner parties for just a dozen close friends at a moment's notice and had white tablecloths and silverware at her picnics. I adored her. She was my heroine; the kind of woman I knew I could never be.

With my very ordinary working-class background, I've always been an impostor in the land of the Volvo Mum. An alien in little gold-barred shoes. I don't like dogs. I don't much like children, either, despite owning four. My children come down to dinner when the smoke alarm goes off and think a ping from the microwave means lunchtime. I had no idea how to be middle class until this blonde highlighted beacon of career motherhood arrived to light my way. I felt if I stood next to her some of her top-drawer boarding-school confidence would transport itself to me. I thought I could possibly learn to be English.

I ached to be like her. I longed to be included in the magic circle of middle-aged matrons called Lulu, Pony, Fifi and Jubby whom she'd known at school. I spent hours perching my bottom on her Aga, the only warm place in her frigid draughty kitchen, blissfully happy in her company. Every invitation was greeted with giddy excitement, only to be followed by a terrible anti-climax as I wondered how long it would be until I saw her again. It was exactly like an adolescent crush. I posed and pirouetted, hoping she'd like me just as much as I did her and even flirted with her husband But there was never any doubt about who I really fancied, and it wasn't the one wearing the faded corduroy trousers.

However, in the end it was all for nothing. She tired of city life, packed up the Mercedes estate and went to live amongst her own kind in the country, leaving me spurned and dejected. Without her example to follow I gave up the fight to become respectable. It was no good. I would never pass. I would never buy ruched curtains and matching bedspreads. I would never learn to say drawing room or wear a taffeta frock in a society magazine. Disheartened, I threw away the velvet hair band and stopped forcing myself to wear navy blue.

It was total agony. But I'm not the only person to suffer from unrequited love. A friend once conducted a long, clandestine affair with a man married to a pretty and talented fashion journalist whose wife she had admired from afar for years. He would make illicit phone calls and ask her what colour underwear she was wearing. In return she'd ask him whether or not his wife dyed her hair. Did she really think you can wear pink fishnet tights with stilettos? And what about leopard skin – trashy or not? It quickly became apparent that she was more interested in his wife than him. She thought if she slept with him then she could miraculously transform herself into the same kind of successful, glamorous person that she imagined his wife to be. When the man eventually offered to leave his marriage, it suddenly struck her that in the end she'd be left with just him and the wife would walk. She might live happily ever after with the husband, but she really wanted to marry the wife.

Of course being infatuated with another woman isn't really about wanting to swap lives. Nor is it necessarily a negation of your own talents and qualities. Rather it's an attempt to complement your life with some attribute that you feel you lack. What you could be if only you were more popular, or more confident, or – in the case of my adulterous friend's wife – if you had trophy hair, a trust fund, invitations to the Chanel sample sales and your own prime-time television show.

It's admiration, not envy. A clear case of projection, but not necessarily perfection. You don't think they have everything sorted, you just admire the way they live their life. My friend Claire currently has a crush on a woman she sees every week at church. She just likes looking at her in fascination, wondering what kind of person she is. When I said I knew her and started filling Claire in on the details, she stopped me. She didn't want me to take away the woman's mystique.

Another friend, Ella, a frequent girlfriend fancier, says that though she enjoys and craves emotional intimacy with other women, 'It's not that you idolise them as much as appreciate their style. It's like when you're a kid and you think – when I grow up I'm going to be just like that. You want some of their verve or their flair, but you want to do it your way. You want character enhancements, not a personality transplant. And anyway, you don't want to be...

The envious friend You know the feeling. You've bought a new dress and you've walked past the mirror several times as if it was an old friend you had just happened to bump into, whilst repeatedly expressing surprise at your gorgeous self, reflected back in the glass. Then you go out to a party and meet someone whose life mission is to find your bubble of self-satisfaction and burst it.

'Love the dress,' she says.

'Oh thanks,' you reply, resisting the impulse to give a little game-show-hostess twirl.

'You're sooooooo lucky to be able to wear that colour,' she says, wincing as though she's in the second stage of labour.

'Well not really,' you answer, trying to offer a whiff of emotional anaesthetic. 'I mean, orange always makes me look a little sallow and it shows all the bumps and lumps.'

The envious friend looks relieved. You're right, after some reflection she thinks it does make you look a little jaundiced. What a shame you paid so much money for it.

But she heard that you'd got engaged/married/pregnant. She bites her lip and flinches. 'You really are soooo lucky.'

Poor thing, this woman needs an epidural of the envy glands and since you've always been a caring sort of person you provide reassurance that marriage/engagement/pregnancy is a hard pill to swallow. In fact the wonder husband keeps ferrets, the fiance whistles Yankee Doodle through his loose fillings and babies smell.

But, you have just broken the cardinal rule of one-upmanship. Reveal nothing and deny everything. The envious friend oozes amazement at your luck and then waits for you to reassure her by rubbishing your own life. Feeling guilty, you divest anything enviable.

The envious friend then goes on her way, serene in the knowledge that the world is a safe place to be for the have-nots but you, my dear, have been strip-searched and exposed. The dress is, after all, a horrible rag – you look like a satsuma that's been sitting at the back of the fridge since 1975. You're not sure why you ever got married, your fiancé's whistling (which you previously thought cute) is driving you mad, and you remember that you don't even like babies.

The only sensible precaution you can take against the 'oh so luckies' amongst your acquaintances is simple. The next time someone begins to tell you that you are 'oh soooo lucky', just smile sweetly, look amazed, as though the idea had never occurred to you before, and agree. Congratulate them on their perception and walk away. Do not, repeat not, confess that your fabulous black patent boots pinch your toes, or that you haven't had sex since George Michael was the lead singer of Wham.

Let her think you have the perfect life. Keep it polished and give it to her to put on her mantelpiece.

The needy friend We've all got a high-maintenance friend with low-rent problems. Her boyfriends look like she's picked them up in a bar after someone else has wiped the counter with them first. They may have a wife, a girlfriend, three children from three different mothers. They might be between jobs or be unpublished writers, struggling artists or unemployed actors who are just waiting for their big break. What they all have in common is the needy friend. The needy friend's love life is a train disaster for which you are required to provide first aid – usually in the middle of the night, and at least twice on Sundays. You need to kiss her better, put her confidence in a splint and slap a band aid on her broken heart. You need to listen.

Of course you don't mind. You are happy to lend a sympathetic ear when she confides in you for the seventh time that her current boyfriend has crossed his cheating heart and promised, this time, definitely to leave his wife. And, of course, you can hardly tell her to shut up, even at 3 a.m., when she calls you up saying that he has changed his mind.

The needy friend is often sad. She sometimes gets depressed. Her life is a mess though it can look as though she had planned it that way. She cries. A lot. You worry about her and make an effort to include her in your social circle. You ask her round for pizza and a video on Saturday evening so she isn't relegated to single hell on a dating night, but if there are no boys coming she invariably cancels at the last minute when she gets a better offer, or one with a Y chromosome. You get your friends to send her invitations to parties where you know there will be spare men. She rarely turns up because the moron of the moment makes a Dr Love house call instead. But if she does show, she stands on the sidelines with an I-don't-know-anyone, poor-little-me look on her face, then leaves with a man she has only just met, and who she is in love with by the next morning.

The needy friend is always in love. Suddenly the phone will go silent. Your direct line to her neuroses will fail to ring. Instead of having to provide four-hourly feeds for her ego, you don't hear from her in four weeks. There are no more cosy chats, no more character-building exercises, you fear she might possibly have killed herself in a fit of rejected pique. You leave messages on her answer phone and text RUOK?s to her cellphone, but to no avail. Love takes all her energy, and man pleasing all her time. So, eventually you give up thinking that it doesn't matter if she isn't in touch, as long as she's happy. And then he dumps her.

Send out the ambulance.

She says things like:

• 'Why aren't you returning my calls?' – when she has rung once, earlier in the day – after months of silence – and you didn't immediately get back to her.
• 'Why are you ignoring me?' – after she rings again (having rung every other name in her address book one after the other and told

them her tale of woe – the Ancient Mariner one-in-three unburdening mode) the same evening and you still haven't called back.

- 'Do you hate me?' – at lunch time the next day, after she has read in a teen magazine with an exclamation mark somewhere in the title, that failing to field two phone calls means that person is no longer your friend. It doesn't occur to her that you're in hospital after being half eaten by your fellow passengers when your plane crashed in the Andes.

She sobs, Tell me the truth – do I look fat? Which, of course, means do not approach the vicinity of the truth even with a baseball cage and a long bat. Not because she is fat – you both know she is a walking French Fry without the ketchup, but because she is like a priest saying a mass, and all you have to do is give the proper responses:

- Do I look fat? – congregation: no you do not look fat.
- Do you think I'm pretty? – congregation: yes, you are very pretty.
- Do you think I'm stupid? – congregation: no you are not stupid.
- Do you really think I'm pretty? – congregation: yes, you are really, really pretty.
- Are you sure you don't hate me? – congregation: yes (though by this point frankly the congregation is getting a little pissed) I'm sure I do not hate you.

    Peace be with you – and with you.

This goes on with only minimum conversational requirements from the listener. Until the needy friend hangs up you need only make soothing noises, tell her that, of course, 'he was a creep', 'I hear you', and say 'uh huh' a few times. This is why women become therapists. They practise for free on their girlfriends. However, with a counselling qualification you also get money.

    But one thing the needy friend never asks is, 'And how are you?'

    So if you are lying in a hospital bed with your legs chewed off, and the rest of your friends are dead or eaten, I hope you brought plenty to read.

On Being Faithful

The happy friend According to current wisdom, every girl needs a gay guy amongst her closest friends. I have had a few myself, though obviously not in the biblical sense, but I'm still not sure about this one. Gay men are no different from straight women – they come in all shapes and sizes with a personality to match. If you find some to suit you, then snap them up as fast as you can. If you don't – there's no obligation.

My current GBF – gay best friend, Timbo – is about ten years younger than I am, carries a satchel across his chest Amazon-style, like a motorcycle courier, wears trousers with lots of zips and is so pierced he looks as though he has perforations. He said he has never met another girl who has had more dodgy sexual liaisons than myself – in fact, he assures me, I could easily be gay. Of course, I'm a woman. He doesn't know our capacity to exaggerate for effect. And he doesn't know many women.

However, from his shambolic personal appearance, he at least puts paid to the old chestnut about gay guys being neat – worrying, if that's our only criteria for deciding whether or not your sons are going to go the way of Sam rather than Samantha. It's in the genes – but it doesn't matter whether they're torn, ripped or crumpled. Though studded leather with detachable jockstrap might offer a clue.

Gay men are supposed to be the arbiters of good taste. They're very big in fashion, but do not rise in any other area featuring women – no matter how hard you try to lure them on to the straight path. But given that one of my friends is a female impersonator who works in a drag club, his masculinity carefully strapped out of sight underneath his gold lamé gown, though I can applaud his Barbra Streisand routine, I don't care much for his frocks. He likes big hair, big wigs, big falsies and gets his thrills from frills. Does he really think we look like that? Say it isn't so. There's only so far you can go with sisterhood when the man prefers a parody woman to you.

However, the whole absence of horny hormones is something of a relief in a relationship with a man of the third sex. No matter how drunk you get, you never smooch into the embarrassing place of no return and sleep with him, thus ruining a perfectly good friendship. You can talk about feelings all night and never get yours hurt.

Another friend, the undisputed holder of the title of World's Kindest Man, was the sweetest and most generous person I knew. He had homes scattered across the French countryside and was so free with his hospitality that often he didn't know the people staying there – but he welcomed them anyway. His house in the Dordogne became known on the hippy trail – like *The Beach* but with sheep. All one had to do was go to the village, find Madame Le Brun and ask for the key and settle oneself down for the summer. And though his own tastes ran to husky men in uniforms, when he visited me in Scotland he entertained us all on New Year's Eve with French love songs – which given our linguistic skills might have been Hawaiian for all anyone knew – followed by the dance of the seven headscarves, when he stripped to reveal a borrowed swimsuit, wearing a pair of citrus breasts. Now, why is it that, sooner or later, it all comes back down to fruit? But I loved his lemons anyway – it didn't make a darn bit of difference that I wasn't interested in squeezing them. And my parents adored him, seeing nothing amiss in his little cabaret act. They just thought he had a lovely baritone – though I should add that by this point in the evening my uncle was in his wife's frock singing 'One Enchanted Evening'.

There are those who say that some gay men don't even like women. And that's news? Some straight men don't like women, yet we still insist on falling in love with them. Hell, some women don't like women. You can't generalise and you shouldn't try. However, my problem with the whole gay guy/girlfriend thing is the rule that we all need one to help us accessorise our outfits.

True, some of them do give good head at the hairdressers and, if you have the body of a prepubescent boy with breasts, they even design fantastic clothes. A friend of mine in LA is a style consultant who dresses men and women who are taste deficient, cash rich, but time poor. He does things like finger the nubby upholstery in your hire car and say, 'Mmm, this colour is to die for.' Then next season, all his clueless clients are wearing car-seat covers.

Why do we need a gay guy to guide us through glamour and criticise our fashion faux pas – hello, sailor, don't we have enough women to do that? Face it, even if they love your sense of style – they do not fancy you. Are you really going to let a man, who under no possible circumstances will ever find you sexually attractive, tell you that your bum is too big?

The nice girl But I guess, everyone still wants to be liked – and the most successful way of attaining it is by being a girl's girl – the kind of person who goes out of her way to bond and be agreeable.

This usually means not being too thin, not being too successful, not being too happily married when everyone else is single (unless the husband in question is certifiably boring and has two chins), not being single when everyone else is married (except miserably so), and certainly not being anything more than passably pretty.

It means ignoring the man sitting on your right at a dinner party and instead spending all your time talking to his mother, his sister or his female flatmate – knowing that if she likes you, you'll get asked back. If you monopolise the man, unless it's love at first sight, he won't ask for your number or even remember your name. If you bond with his sister, she'll tell him your name and write it on his arm.

Nice girls behave the selfless way débutantes were taught to act in order to catch a husband. But now that husbands come and go, friends are a better long-term investment. So they smile a lot and look terribly interested even if you're only reciting the contents of your fridge backwards. They don't talk about their job but gush appreciatively about yours. They love babies and are fascinated by the night feeds and the consistency of sick. They love hearing about your holidays, your boyfriend problems, your plastic surgery and your post-natal depression. They will, however, confess neuroses similar to your own in order to complete a successful game of emotional ping pong where you've both cared and shared. Nice girls offer to babysit, they take your dry cleaning to the laundry and water your plants when you're away – even if you hardly know them. They're doormats but they make you feel safe, loved and accepted by not appearing to be anything of a threat.

Nice girls say things like:

- 'Have you lost weight?' – and look as though they mean it.
- 'Don't be silly, you are not fat' – even if you're pregnant.
- 'But it suits you.' If you are too fat to lie about.
- 'I love your hair that way.'
- 'Those are fabulous shoes.'
- 'Love your handbag.'
- 'No really, I hadn't even noticed it.' When you're sporting a pimple on your chin with its own advertising campaign.
- 'I can't believe you have four children.'

These phrases do have to be used with the proper facial expressions of sincerity. Any hint of sarcasm and you've blown your cover – your under-bitch is showing.

The bitch Now I am not a nice girl. I don't do nice. I can offer my share of heartfelt flattery but if I were a nice person, even a fake nice person I'd be practising my wide-eyed stare of fascination or off taking friend's babies for walks or delivering meals on wheels to the old and infirm. I would not be sitting here in my pyjamas pinching myself to make sure I'm not dead, and ringing myself up on the phone just to check I'm home.

However, there is an agreeable level of self-confessed bitchiness allowed as our birthright and which we will tolerate and even enjoy amongst ourselves. But there's also the kind of bitch who is blissfully unaware that she is not your companion of choice for a three hour lunch. At all costs, beware the bitch who thinks she's being friendly.

One of my husband's relatives has to take the title of Queen Bitch. At my wedding she asked me if I had enjoyed my honeymoon – but meant the one I'd taken some years earlier with a previous husband. She asked me where I got my dress and accent and applauded my courage for wearing both at the same time. She told me the only interesting member of our wedding party was my crazy aunt who spoke to fairies, kept a pet rock and kissed all the photographs on her wall every night before she went to sleep. She may have gone to charm school, but she was better with snakes than with people and she was so pretentious that although her name was Fiona she spelled it with a 'Ph'.

My own bitchiness is a sleeping tiger, easily roused – though possibly rather geriatric and arthritic in that I can only think of the stinging reply long after the other person has walked off. It's like school netball all over again. I always knew what I was supposed to do with the ball, but every time it was passed to me, I dropped it. These childhood traumas scar one, you know. Isn't that how the bitch is born? Women like cousin Phiona are probably just terribly unhappy, frustrated, lost foundlings who strike out like a hissing cobra before you attack them first.

Women like me are just slow on the uptake – and very bad at ball games.

There's the girlfriend-moment bitch as in 'can we just have a girlfriend moment?' She'll call you over, confidentially – as though she had a problem only you can solve. You go, smilingly naively, expecting a juicy piece of gossip – something like her confessing a lifelong sadomasochistic impulse to pull out her own hair. But what she really wants to talk about is your brand new rent-a-tart, see-them-and-drool sandals. She looks at you, purses her lips and says, 'You know , those shoes just don't work – they make your feet look big.'

Similar girlfriend moments might include the following:

- 'You don't suit that colour.'
- 'I really don't like that bag.'
- 'I love the dress but the style is all wrong on you.'
- 'Oh, what a shame about your hair.'

What I'd really like them to tell me is where the word 'friend' comes into any of these statements. Who the hell asked them for their self-treasured opinion? Do I need to know my lovely, lovely shoes were a mistake? Does it make me happy? Does it enrich my life and fill me with Louis Vuiton-monogrammed bags of confidence? It's not a girlfriend moment, it's an act of war. But it's a war you won't win if you retaliate. The girlfriend who blithely tells you she doesn't like your scarf will burst into tears of hurt disbelief if you try her own approach on her. She won't thank you for sharing that she looks like a Bolivian peasant on steroids in her new floaty blouse. Even bitches bleed.

This kind of girlfriend takes over where your mother left off, telling you in the spirit of kinship just exactly what you don't need to know. Face it, if you want criticism your mother still doesn't know there's a vacancy – she's been doing a great job of telling it like it is for most of your life:

- 'You're not going out looking like that are you?'
- 'Did you pay someone to do that to your hair?'
- 'Humph.'

That 'Humph' says everything. Your mother is a professional who doesn't even need words to convey her disapproval. And she doesn't need an assistant.

The bitch who cannot tell a lie In friendship, I feel that honesty is overrated. Okay, you don't want to be the sycophantic nice girl, halfway up your friend's inside leg with your tongue extended, but there's a subtle difference between the eager-to-please yes girl and the I-love-you-too-much-to-hurt-your-feelings friend. A bit of obfuscation goes a long way to ensuring an enduring friendship. People who begin their sentences with:

- Frankly
- To be honest
- If you want the truth

are fine if they're standing up in court testifying to the stoutness of your character, but not when they're talking about your physical appearance. When they're telling you anything about your complexion, your boyfriend or your clothes they should just shut the hell up. The bitch who cannot tell a lie should be locked up naked in a mirrored room with the girlfriend-moment bitch and left until they're both feeling low enough to crawl underneath the door.

Don't be Frank – be Arthur, George or Henry. And – d'you know what? (another prelude to an unwelcome observation) – I don't want the truth. I can see the truth for myself. I want some well-meaning lies. I don't need to hear that you think my friend from college is shallow or that my father looks like a hall porter. I want to hear palatable untruths so I can go on living with the size of my hips and the fact that when my roots grow in my head looks like a badger's bum. And though I don't insist on perjury a few pleasant platitudes never go amiss.

The truth hurts. The truth rubs lemon juice into an ego that is already superficially scraped. The person sharing the truth, holding it high like the bloody Statue of Liberty's torch to illuminate your shortcomings might well think she's taking the chairlift straight up the moral snow-topped mountain with her uncompromising morality. Actually, she's a pain in the Aspens. When did God die and leave your best friend in charge of fashion? Yes, your Moschino belt might be vulgar and not ironic as you try to pretend, but does it matter? Will they be crying in heaven because you're wearing more gilt letters than a gangsta' rapper? Will there never be peace in the Middle East as long as you wear coloured nail varnish instead of having a French manicure? I think not.

These people treat the truth, or their version of it, as though it was a big stick to beat you over the head with. Then, when you protest, they say you're full of anger and beat you some more. The truth hurts and you're not even allowed to scream. Does it help to be told that someone is jealous of you? That your colleague at work thinks you are silly and impressionistic? Oh, no, please let's not be Frank. Let's just be Pollyanna.

There are many truths – yours, mine and your mother's. Even the president is allowed to bend it a little. So if I ask someone, 'Do you like my hair?' the answer I'm hoping for does not begin with N and end with O. Obviously, a person asking this sort of question knows there might be a problem with the hair and is therefore desperately seeking reassurance, not a poke in the guts with the sharp truth.

The bitch in drag is wearing a pained smile, pretending to sound concerned about you. She says things like:

• 'You look tired.' When everyone knows that looking tired is a euphemism for looking rougher than a sailors armpit.

• 'You look well.' Do not be deceived – she means fat.

• 'You look pale.' Another purportedly well-intended comment that means either you're wearing too much foundation, or you look tired, ill or dead.

• 'You're too thin.' No one has said this to me in twenty years, but it's a phrase that fatties use towards women who have been on a successful diet to make them feel self-conscious and anorexic.

It's absolutely forbidden – unless you like being smacked in the mouth with a fully loaded handbag – ever to come right out and say that someone – no matter how obese – actually looks fat, but it's considered perfectly acceptable to make pitying comments about someone whose bones you can see. Of course it's passive aggression disguised as sympathy. Unless you're talking Callista Flockhart or Posh Spice, who definitely need to put some flesh on their frame lest someone mistakes them for a snack at a cocktail party and eats them.

But even amongst women who look like emaciated chickens, if they're truly body dysmorphic, no amount of fake concern is going to with convince them that they don't look like the fat lady in the circus. And if they do realise but – shock, horror, are naturally skinny – it's kinder to say nothing. I know. I was mistaken for a boy until I was twenty, and if I stood still for any length of time people would chain their dogs to my legs. Believe it or not, the words 'Belsen' and 'Prisoner of War' do not do much for a teenager's confidence.

'Poor you' is a catch-all response to any admission of failure, disappointment or personal disaster. Mugs often mix these women up with someone who really gives a damn – and tell them all sorts of stories about cheating boyfriends, bullying bosses and borderline personality disorders.

My mother used to say that you find out who your friends are in the bad times. This is true, but you will also find out who your friends are when you change your life for the better. You can moan at national level and the bitch in drag loves you – but God forbid you want to tell her about your success. Then you're 'full of yourself' and she doesn't want to hear it. It doesn't know how to say 'well done' – it's not in her phrase book. When the going gets good – the grumblers get going – looking to find another struggling soul to feel sorry for.

'Don't take this the wrong way' is another phrase that should have you closing your ears and running for cover. Recently I've been told:

- 'Don't take this the wrong way but you could be ugly – though you're not.'

- 'Don't take this the wrong way but since I met you I've discovered just how shallow the world of food writing really is.'

Now – what is the right way to take either of these statements. Pleasure? Spontaneous applause? Writing gift next to their name on your Christmas card list? I don't think so.

The level of anger that women can show towards each other is staggering. I've already mentioned 'You've lost weight, I hate you', but what about:

- 'She's so thin I could kill her.'
- 'She's so pretty you want to punch her.'
- 'All the girls in my office are so young and clever that I want to grind glass into their faces.'

What ever happened to friendship?

The good friends Why do sitcoms about a gay guy and a straight girl sharing a flat together, a collection of unlovely, oddball New Yorkers or six trendy twenty-something metropolitans living across the hall from each other so capture the nation's imagination? It's because most of us don't live like that.

Yes, we have friends and work colleagues, but they live on the other side of town. We have families – but they usually live in another country. And as for neighbours – we wait till they leave the building so we don't have to talk to them. We see our friends once a week if we're lucky and our relationship consists of text messages or bleeps left on the other person's answerphones. Our social life consists of making dates, then breaking them and making another so that in six months you've played telephone tag, had three good intentions to go to lunch, but not actually clapped eyes on each other. Some of us even have groups of friends who hang out together – but God forbid that everyone should actually get on. Admit it – you hate your best friend's boyfriend, the two girls you went to college with annoy you, and you know your boyfriend's sister really thinks you're bad for her brother. Half the time our friends don't mix because although you may find them congenial, none of them like each other..

It's so much more simple to watch your TV friends walk in and out of each other's apartments, helping themselves to each other's snacks, opening the fridge and drinking all the soda, monopolising the television – hanging out on the sofa with a take away pizza (which judging by their figures they throw up again immediately afterwards) than having to put up with your own friends doing the same. For prospective visitors to my house – if you open the fridge to get out milk for your coffee you'll be forgiven, but if you touch the Diet Coke, I'll kill you.

Another thing that makes it difficult to keep up with your friends is a particularly virulent form of the social disease, mostly prevalent in cities, called Cancellitis.

The fairweather friend who takes a raincheck It strikes without warning, though it does tend to afflict the same people over and over again.

I'm not a sufferer myself – I'm one of those saddos with a healthy open-air diary that never gets full which means I can invariably get through a whole year cancel free. I'm the dullard who makes a date and sticks to it. Mother Teresa of the appointment book – I juggle trivial inconveniences like head injuries, minor house fires and the odd car accident so that I can stick to my plans without letting anyone down.

But just as I've come home from the supermarket laden with shopping, begged a few extra chairs from a neighbour and arranged the flowers – the phone rings and one of the guests comes down with Cancellitis.

The symptoms vary – sometimes the disease presents with a rash of no-show babysitters or sick-child syndrome – infants who can't be left at home in case their mosquito bite turns out to be smallpox. But often it's just a really bad case of change-your-minditis accompanied by fatigue.

Secondary symptoms, such as colds, backache, migraine and sudden onset gastro-enteritis often occur with the first signs of excuses offered with a weak, slightly feeble voice. And I have come across the somewhat rarer Cancellitis by proxy, when sufferers get someone else to ring up and cancel for them. This is common in schoolchildren but is almost eradicated by adulthood.

I can't remember a single case of it while I lived at home with my parents but nowadays we live such stressful lives that social engagements which seemed like such a good idea three months earlier, feel like too much effort when you're exhausted. So come home from work. You crumble. You cancel.

We've all had a mild case of it from time to time, but some people are chronic sufferers. Someone I know cancelled because she and her boyfriend had had an argument and she couldn't face coming to dinner. She then added, oh and don't tell anyone why I can't come – just make up some excuse. Charming, since I'd planned the whole evening for her boyfriend's dietary requirements and only asked the other guests because they were people she wanted to meet.

Cheek, I must add, often presents itself at the same time as Cancellitis.

Another couldn't-be-arsed friend recently left a message on my answerphone cancelling lunch because her glands were swollen and she needed to rest. I then met her, at lunchtime, in the supermarket where she was doing the family shop. I had gone in to get her some flowers.

Some cases are genuine, but a qualified hostess can usually spot these and treat them with kindly understanding. Otherwise, forewarned is forearmed. Early warning signs to look out for are unpunctuality and failure to return phone calls. All suspected my-life-is-much-more-important-than-yours tendencies should be treated with suspicion. Guest-list vetting and last-minute better invitationitis can also occur and are especially prevalent amongst heavy duty networkers.

Cancellitis, no matter how much it hurts, must always be taken incredibly lightly. You must be brave and say, 'Oh, please don't worry about it.' Other suitable responses are 'It couldn't matter less', 'Take care of yourself', 'Get better soon', 'Do let me know if there's anything I can do' (usually said through gritted teeth) and 'Don't apologise, we'll do it another time'.

To react otherwise makes you look like a pathetic loser with no friends, no life, and an unhealthy desire to see people who have no respect for you.

So if your best friends are all known sufferers you either have to persevere, or try to find some non-afflicted new friends.

Alternatively, cancel first.

The thankless friend Whatever happened to the social nicety of the thank-you letter? They are becoming collector's items – so rare that I'd be grateful to have just one – even if it wasn't mine.

Don't get me wrong, I'm never going to win any prizes for hostess of the year, but on the rare occasion when I do push the party boat out, I'm continually stunned by how few people ever bother to do so much as call to say they've enjoyed themselves. It's as if your friends feel that bringing a lukewarm bottle of inferior Romanian red which someone brought to their last dinner party is enough of a thank you. Or maybe they're expecting you to write and thank them for the wine.

But thankless friends are only the tip of the social iceberg – there are the friends who come repeatedly for dinner but never ask you back. Then there are the friends who do ask you back but for a kitchen supper of microwave pizza with no other guests after you've thrown a gala event in their honour. There are the friends who offer you carbonated water and put your bottle of champagne in the fridge to enjoy alone later. And then there are the friends who come to dinner and don't even bother with the wine.

Because I am a lady who lunches, I regularly take people with me on my various restaurant reviews. Admittedly, I am not paying for these meals myself – I have an expense account, but it certainly feels as though it's coming out of my personal bank account when I have to wait up to two months to get it reimbursed.

In the land of the free lunch it's amazing how many people start with a glass of champagne, have the whole spectrum of wines, an aged brandy and even a cigar, yet don't feel they have to be appreciative. I expect they feel, since it's on my employer's tab, that they owe me no social obligation. Indeed they think they've done me an enormous favour by agreeing to come out with me.

But then I've always had to buy my friends.

With your intimate best buddies, of course, there's no need to thank them every time they make you a cup of coffee and a sandwich, at least not on embossed notepaper, hand delivered by a flunky the next day. It would be like television tennis – back and forth so frequently that you would soon forget whose turn it was to pick up the ball and lob it back. However, I still feel that it is only good manners to pull out your pen when the occasion demands. Three courses with pudding and cheese is one such occasion. The wedding present, thoughtfully chosen from the bride and groom's pre-vetted list of items containing nothing under £50, another. The birthday present, the baby shower gift, the flowers, the kind note sent when your father dies – all deserve some sort of reciprocity.

Of course mothers are supposed to sit you down after Christmas and force you to write out painstaking thank-you letters, which may well be why, later in life, we pass the envelope and don't bother. But you should – the only gift that does not require a thank you is herpes. In this case you might consider writing instead to each of the bestower's acquaintances including employees and workmates, to spread the word of their generosity.

Naturally, I always write and say thank you – some time during the course of the next calendar year, in which case one note can cover a number of occasions. So correct am I about thank-you notes that I tend to carry them about in my handbag unposted for months – because I feel deprived. I obviously suffer from banal retention – hugging those bread-and-butter letters to my heart. I then make a point of phoning my thank yous, at 7.30 on a Sunday morning, before I forget and the notion goes out of my head like low-lather shampoo.

E-mail is the modern way – who can resist the curt one-line message with it's charming misspellings, lack of ceremony and of punctuation? It's truly heartwarming. I, however, try to avoid the e-thank you.

I try to avoid e-mail altogether.

The anonymous friend I used to be a disciple at the First Church of On-Line Confession. I had an e-mail account before there was anyone to send messages to, but when I found a few correspondents it was a revelation. Had I had it several years ago I might have done without at least the first of my husbands – there are much better things to do on the Internet than marry a man who thinks that a Vindaloo on a Saturday night is an ancient Indian form of foreplay.

Initially, I loved it, but recently I'm afraid I've lost my religion. As far as I'm concerned you can stuff the information superhighway. You can dig it up, close off all three lanes, fill the hard shoulder with bollards and install a sign permanently flashing, 'Warning! congestion ahead, find alternative route' because, believe me, e-mail bites. And it has very sharp teeth.

I never quite saw the point of surfing the net. In the beginning I paddled a bit, dipped my toe into the murky waters of the World Wide Web. For a while it's grand to read a daily newspaper from every major city in the world – and be bored in seventeen languages, including Esperanto, without leaving the comfort of your own home.

But what are all those websites actually for? Sure it's nice to look at photographs of best friend Julia's new baby (www.sweetweething.com) – but I can't understand why Coca Cola has a home page. If you want a drink you go to the fridge and get one. You don't navigate your way through endless screens of flickering text, and then wait ten minutes to download a picture of a can of coke.

And chat rooms – there's a misnomer if ever there was one. When not full of little kids saying 'Wow – cool!' there's not a whole lot of chatting going on. It's either like visiting an on-line gay bath house, or populated by inane, monosyllabic people repeatedly asking, 'Is anybody there?'

We've all heard of the e-mail affair, a subject I will touch on under its proper heading – madness – but one should not forget the e-mail friendship, the e-mail misunderstanding and the e-mail quarrel. Initially, during my e-mail conversion, I enjoyed a sporadic correspondence with several old acquaintances now languishing in academic establishments around the world, all with tenure and free access to the internet. I even had the occasional list of building specifications from my brother, an engineer in the Virgin Islands, a man unfortunately not always in touch with his feelings.

However, I soon discovered that the real reason I lost contact with all those great friends was that I didn't actually like them all that much. In their youth they might have been the crème de la crème but the years have soured them somewhat. Knowing their e-mail address did not change them into someone I wanted to talk to.

Nor they, it seems, me.

Those of you who know my pacific and gentle disposition will be surprised to hear that over the last three years I have managed to offend no fewer than two journalists, a Professor of

Greek Studies, A lecturer in Middle East Politics, an Associate Professor of Agriculture and Soil Science, my old au-pair now living in San Francisco, Ms Manless in Mexico, Ms Depressed in Illinois, several members of husband's extended family and even my damn brother.

It appears it is possible to 'shout' on-line without realising you've raised your voice, and to be 'snappish' merely by a 'slip' of the typing finger. As a result I find myself totally friendless in cyberspace.

What makes this even worse is the prevalence of e-spite on the web. It's perfectly lovely to get a message from someone who sees your name on a bulletin board or to join a virtual conversation in a chat room (if you're twelve) – it's a lot less fun getting an unsigned missive from a nutter in Dakota who likes dogs more than is healthy. And it's downright horrible getting a virus called I Love You that wipes out your hard disk. It is even possible to be sent a virtual bouquet of dead roses without knowing the donor, their age or their location. All you do know is that someone out there really doesn't like you. These people don't mind sharing their sexual foibles or wacky politics, but never their name.

People who would never consider sending an anonymous letter through the post will happily send an e-mail. Yes, there's always a return address – usually something unattributable – from Yahoo or Hotmail, often a symbol instead of a name like ?@Udon'tknowme.com. But this offers no clues to who this person is – they might call themselves Heidi from Bora Bora but they could be Henry with the binoculars in the room across the block.

Perversely, you don't care if they call themselves John the Baptist if they are writing to say something innocuous, but it leaves a bad taste in your mouth when it's all about your short tenure on the planet or the sender's enthusiasm for water sports – and I'm not talking water ski-ing.

Tone can be a problem in e-mail. It's like a phone call that you can re-read. You can be brusque on the phone, but two seconds later the other person has hung up and forgotten. With an on-line message you have time to pore over it and wonder what exactly they meant by a seemingly casual phrase. It's easy to sound offhand when you meant to be ironic, or snappy when you are merely hurried, but Long John Dong 10 has usually only one meaning.

So I don't want any more anonymous pen pals. I want a letter with an address at the top and a signature at the bottom. Come out and show yourself. Put a first-class stamp where your mouth is.

And learn to spell.

The real friend Your mother might have encouraged you to play with the good little girl with bows on her shoes who ate chocolate wearing white gloves and a banana with a knife and fork – but back then she thought it was good manners, not worrying Freudian behaviour. But the real friend is no little Miss Perfect. You like her better when she sharpens the knife and the gloves are off. The real friend is all of the above. Sometimes she's a class A Bitch who should be kept in a locked cabinet. Sometimes she's a sweet, self-effacing Rebecca of Sunnybrook Farm and a sickening suck-up, while at other times she's gossiping about you with all your other friends agreeing that – yes – really you are a witch without transport.

You take what you want from your friends and ignore the bits you don't like (such as their horrible boyfriend), and trust that they will do the same for you. You learn to accept their foibles. You understand that when a friend asks you where you got your sweater and then buys exactly the same one it's meant to be flattering – even when she boasts that it's a smaller size. And if you know it isn't – you keep quiet. They call you when you drop out of sight, they help you move. You help them decorate.

Good friends never judge you. They listen to what you have to say but never offer advice based on their own experiences, even when you ask for it. Your problems can only be solved in your context – not theirs. But the best friends offer sympathy whenever necessary, and a good kick up the backside when you're feeling sorry enough for yourself already. They cannot always be magnanimous enough to be proud of you or pleased about your successes, but they swallow their envy like a wad of chewed out flavourless bubble gum and congratulate you anyway. And they are never happy when you fail. They call your facial mole a beauty spot and you describe their six stomachs as voluptuous. They say you're vivacious, not garrulous. They confess, confide and while they're doing it you provide alcohol and tissues, and you shut up and listen. They never pass on things other people say about you pseudo-sympathetically as 'bad news' but will always make a point of repeating the compliments. Good friends talk you up – they don't do you down. They are every bitch and all woman, and, as my 'what's that muck you're wearing on your face, can't say I'm keen on this casserole, isn't it time you gave your hair a wash' mother always says, if they can't say something good, they say nothing.

My mum was never big on compliments, so it was usually pretty quiet around our house. But having a little complimentary love-fest with your friends is one of the perks of the job.

Until you fall out.

The ex-friend Oh yes, friendship sours and infatuation fizzles. Just like a love affair, attraction burns itself out. One day you discover you just don't feel the same way. What you once saw as confidence starts to look suspiciously like smugness, and the ironic sense of humour you used to enjoy begins to feel like black do-yourself-down negativity.

Or worse. She dumps you. She's evasive. She never returns your calls. She spends so much time washing her hair that you're surprised she has any left, and she's busier in the evenings than a Bangkok hooker.

It hurts. It hurts like hell and – unlike breaking up with a man – you know that this has nothing to do with sex. It's not about fear of commitment or the noise of your biological clock ringing like a whole call centre of unanswered phones. It's honest-to-God, one-hundred per cent personal. She just doesn't like you any more.

We've all been dumped, abandoned and forgotten. When my once upon a time bestest friend ever, Jane, moved with her family to Kenya it felt like a bereavement and it was months before I could even bring myself to say her name out loud without sobbing. Losing her was like losing an arm. Some endings are like acrimonious divorce where months after you've stopped seeing them you're still quibbling about who was right, who was wrong and who has your Armani jeans. I have lots of practice at losing friends. They're like good jewellery – you mean to take better care of them but sooner or later a ring just slips off, or you lose the matching earring. You offend them. You sleep with their boyfriend. Their boyfriend sleeps with your husband. They have impossible double standards which you can't live up to or they bore you to death.

But on the whole they are easier to come by than husbands and live-in lovers. You have different friends for different reasons. The dull dependables, the exciting glamorous ones, the work friends, the hangers-on from college, the ones who never ask you to dinner but you like anyway because they're entertaining and the ones you only see because they insist on inviting you round and you don't know how to say no.

So, yes it's sad when a friendship goes belly up and you feel like the orange cream that no one except old people with dentures wants to eat. But you get over it. You get over everything in time. And if you don't, you can always just get a cat.

Your feline friend There's nothing sadder than a woman of a certain age with a cat. Dogs are somehow seen as more rugged – unless they look like beribboned ferrets and you can keep them in your handbag – then, frankly, you're sub sad. But cat people cannot be seduced away from their kitties – at Christmas they send you kitty cards and give you cartoon kitty mugs, cushions and novelty ties. The cat is their friend, their companion, their baby. And though dogs might be butch, cats have more character. Dogs are faithful and friendly, like the kind of well-trained man that we all think we want but know would drive us barking mad. Cats are snitchy, bitchy, contrary, independent creatures with characters and minds – and answerphones – of their own. A dog comes when you call it. A cat will get back to you. If it feels like it.

Single girls keep cats so there is someone to rub their legs against at night when they come home to an otherwise empty apartment. They have kittens to satisfy their thwarted maternal urges. At least I'm assuming it's not because they just adore the scent of kitty litter and cat pee hanging over their apartments like Eau de Spinster – and believe me, despite what you might think, cats – just like your own gaseous emissions – do smell, even if you think they don't. Cats don't borrow your make-up, laugh at your hair, talk back, gossip or tell you you look fat. However they do puke on the rug, rip your tights and ignore you with alacrity. But if you do something they don't like at least they don't whine about it. They just scratch you instead. You know where you are with a cat – and if they do sleep with your boyfriend, you really don't mind.

It's an established fact that people also get pets when their breeding days are over. If all your friends are having babies and it proves impossible to resist the urge to procreate a little late in the day, you either decide to having another baby yourself – or you get an animal.

It happened to me. How could I not envy all the elderly prima gravidas finally getting their biological act together and producing the much longed-for baby? I tormented myself with thoughts of returning to the early days of gummy smiles, sweet helplessness and Johnson's baby powder instead of a pair of stroppy teenagers who stink of Lynx aftershave and are only helpless when presented with a sink full of washing up. Yes, yes, the sleepless nights, the haemorrhoids, the varicose veins and the baby-sick worn like a pashmina down the back of your once dry-clean-only sweater which now lives in the continually running washing machine. But in return there's the illusion of being youthfully fertile, an excuse for being fat for at least nine months and a chance to splurge on cute little baby clothes, so much cheaper than a grown-up day at Prada.

If this isn't quite enough cause to suck your thumb and cry for your blankie, even more enviable are the second-time-rounders. These women already have partly grown-up families and are doing it all again with partner number two, three or four. They don't need to buy the kit as they already have all the teeny, tiny baby-grows, packed away in tissue paper. They just buy a new trendy three-wheel buggy and get the old cot down from the attic – though where they get their energy from is quite another matter. Of course you hope that the older children will help with the baby-sitting and that the teenage daughters won't be grossed out by the idea that you are still having sex at your age. Then there are always fathers one and two to take the others off your hands at weekends. And if you close your eyes really, really tightly and try to forget all about labour and stretch marks, you can remember all the other wonderful moments of motherhood that you yearn to relive. The sheer unadulterated joy of bringing a new life home from the hospital, the first (polite) words and the bliss when they finally say 'Mummy' as opposed to later when you hear it for the five-millionth time in one sentence, each preceded by 'but'.

Oh the cuddly toys, and the bathroom littered with rubber ducks instead of arthritis medicine. The soggy kisses and the damp cuddles. The mobiles playing soft, soothing lullabies at bedtime instead of loud music and bedtime a mere fiction in the minds of gullible parents. How can we miss the chance to do it all over again? In our case we thought four children were enough and as I've had him for eighteen years I also lost out on the 'new partner' clause. But we had a baby anyway.

Ours was feline in character and peed in a box by the door, but in most other respects the resemblance was remarkable, with the added bonus that cats also kill pests. They eat the food from the floor as opposed to chucking it there for you to pick up later, curl up on your lap without needing a story and are (almost) toilet trained when you get them. They cry at night and need lots of attention as well as beds, cat-carriers, exercise frames and soft squeaky toys. They also come with a whole stack of literature on caring for your kitten that rivals anything offered by the maternity hospital – of which the most useful words of advice would have been 'Childbirth really hurts and cats don't.'

We chose and discarded names with a Solomonian diplomacy not shown to most children – otherwise who, except those living in Pratsville, would call their son Zeus? We bought flea powder and toothbrushes, pet insurance and scratching posts, and we waited for the happy event.

Sadly, our first kitten got sick and had to go back to its mother, but – hey presto – we just picked out another one instead. Unfortunately you can't do that with babies.

But you can do it with friends when they let you down. So don't take any shit.

Unless it's the cat's.

Sex, Love and Videotaping

When it comes to the facts of life, mothers fall into two categories. There's the kind of mother who would rather drill out her own fillings than mention anything beginning with S and ending with X, (my mother even calls socks hosiery) – and the kind who draws you diagrams with anatomically correct moving parts and insists on pulling all the strings herself.

Thankfully most of us have the first sort – the mother who treats the subject of sex as though it was a wasp at a picnic. She gives it the odd offhanded swat from time to time, tries to ignore it and hopes it will go away, or she runs off screaming and tells us absolutely nothing.

I follow the 'don't ask, don't tell' approach with my own kids, and offer information only on a need-to-know basis. Thanks to school sex-education programs and the sexually implicit content of most television programmes, I haven't had to say much – *Dawson's Creek*, *Friends* and four children have done it all for me. And even I've learned something from *Sex and the City* – though a regular viewer could be forgiven for thinking that keeping your bra on during intercourse was an erotic requirement. All TV sex kittens make love in their nightdresses, thereby missing a few key erogenous zones. In TV land, lingerie is much more important than love.

But not even the most sophisticated, 43-year-old child feels comfortable spending too much time (i.e. any longer than it takes to blink) thinking about their own parents having sex. Like being dragged across gravel by a runaway horse, or where your navel goes when you're seventy, it's something that you don't want to even imagine. The threat of the family sex talk is such an efficient deterrent that I feel prisons should use it against young criminals. Forget probation and reform school – sit them down and force them to maintain eye contact while they listen to their mother and father recounting their top ten sexual experiences – they'll never re-offend.

When my mother decided it was time to discuss the 'birds and bees', she got as far as, 'Well you're getting to be a big girl now' before I yelled, 'I already know everything' and fled to the spare room, where I locked myself in the closet with a tea trolley, my sister's bridesmaid's dress, my father's Masonic sash and a dead fox. Not deliberately, you understand – it wasn't some weird Scottish adolescent rite of passage; it was just that these particular items lived in the cupboard. Only we would keep a tea trolley wedged in a cupboard in an upstairs bedroom where, on no possible occasion, it would be available for use, next to a dress worn only once in 1963 which was fashionable sometime around 1948. When you take into account that the dead fox fur – a poor, supposedly decorative creature with glass eyes, doomed to hold its own tail between its jaws inside a mothbally plastic bag for eternity – was seriously scary and that the bridesmaid's dress was pink nylon tulle and downright terrifying – you can tell how disturbed I was.

And of course, despite my protestations, I knew nothing. Having an older sister meant I was spared the ignominy of imagining my first period was a life-threatening haemorrhage and I was clear on the mechanics. But sex is like building an IKEA wardrobe – knowing that bolt A goes into slot B is the easy part; it's why anyone, especially your mother and father, would want to be bothered doing it in the first place that's difficult to work out.

Nowadays, it's much simpler. You can talk openly about why all the jokes on *Frasier* have gay implications although the characters are all straight, and for the technical details you can buy the kids a lift-the-flap book and let them get on with it.

Alternatively, you can always give them an instruction sheet for the IKEA wardrobe and explain the similarities.

I got most of my early information out of a book. As a pre-teen I was fond of dressing up in the pink bridesmaid's dress, and playing at being the runner-up in the Miss World Contest by wearing my father's Masonic sash draped across my non-existent chest (I could only ever come second, as we had no crown). But after I tired of practising for a life as an also-ran, I'd go rummaging through the drawers in search of my mother's book on pregnancy and childbirth. This was a classic post-war horror story of gynaecological nightmares. After 300 yellowing pages describing organs I didn't even know I possessed such as prolapsed wombs the size of udders and record-breaking fibroids big enough to take first prize at a Gardening Show, came a series of grim line drawings showing the progress of a spectacularly cross baby down the birth canal which looked like a boa constrictor regurgitating its prey. This was followed by an epilogue of birth defects. What better anti-sex aide could a mother wish for than mouldy, damp-spotted pictures of Siamese twins and the baby with two heads? Being second in the Miss World Contest was infinitely more desirable.

As a result of my early ignorance, I have had to grasp the whole question of sex firmly by the ears and educate myself. I have become the sort of woman who furtively completes those quizzes in magazines that ask Are You Satisfying Your Man? and an avid reader of articles entitled 23 Erogenous Zones We've Just Made Up to Get A Headline. I've even read Sex Tips for Straight Women, by a Gay Man – even though, despite the obvious similarities, like we lust after the same gender – we really don't share the same goals. No sirree Bob, we don't.

Whenever I do the quizzes, I always come out with a great sex-kitten score – but how difficult is it to work out that the As are all in 'You are a frigid cow' category and come with a freephone number for a self-help line, the Bs say you're boring in bed and the Cs call you Emmanuelle? But though I'm an expert on all the theory, I rarely do any of the stuff in the boxes I'm ticking. Over the years, naturally I've practised enough, but I still secretly worry that despite knowing all the answers, I have no innate ability. As Larry, a friend of mine who shares the same anxieties, says, 'It's like lacrosse. I'm there on the pitch, and I've got the uniform on and the wee net thingy clasped very firmly in my hand. I know all the rules – but I don't really have the foggiest idea how to play.'

How do you know if you're any good at sex? Well, not by asking your mother. Your mother doesn't want you to have sex until hell freezes over and everyone can ice dance. She would, of course, like grandchildren some day – preferably immaculately conceived – at some time far in the future when she is much too busy to baby-sit but not too old for constructive interference. And while any mother except mine, for whom 'quite nice' is high praise, would be happy to insist that their daughter is without equal, the most skilled, successful, pretty, attractive and talented girl alive – she's going to be uncomfortable having to grade you on sexual technique. Especially if you insist on demonstrating.

You could ask your friends, but since one of my very gorgeous, very eligible, very single friends just called and asked if it was acceptable to get 'frisky' on a first date, I wouldn't be too sure of their level of expertise. 'What do you mean frisky?' I asked. 'Well you know,' she said (I didn't). 'It's been so long since I've been on a date I don't know what men expect any more. I've asked all my girlfriends and none of them know either.'

Nor will you necessarily get a reliable response from your partner.

In the case of allowable friskiness, translated as 'should you sleep with him on the first date?' he'll say,

A) Yes
B) Yes
C) Yes
D) Yes

On the question of being good in bed:

A) He says, yes, you are the best lover he has ever had.
B) He says, hell yes, of course you are the best lover he has ever had.
C) He says, you are the absolutely only lover he has ever had.
D) He says, well, now that you mention it...

D is the wrong answer and means he will never score again, unless he's a masochist and likes having a stiletto heel banged repeatedly against his chest – though according to a quiz I read recently, this is not as uncommon as you might think... A and B are the right answers, but not necessarily sincere. C is a downright lie – either that or you're playing with a man who is still living with his mother aged 56 – or a man still living with his mother aged 16. In both cases you need help, girl, and a quiz isn't where you're going to get the solution to this problem.

While having dinner in a fashionable new restaurant, I did once mention to my dining partner that I feared that my seduction skills were becoming a little rusty. He then proceeded to give a very visual description of two sex acts – one with a bottle of Chateau Musar, and another involving a single pomegranate seed which, given my preference for men over women, was fairly redundant, but nevertheless very enlightening. I recommend you let any prospective lover chase a pomegranate seed round a plate before you let him anywhere near you. Firstly you'll get a jolly good laugh and secondly it might alert him to the fact that although men always complain our major erogenous zones move around like a groupie chasing a rock star, at least he might get an idea of the ball park area.

I was not interested in having this man twiddle any of my dials, and would have stopped him but I suddenly found it quite impossible to find my tongue (I think it was somewhere around my feet). The wine bottle demonstration, however, was very instructive. I hadn't realised it was such a complex operation, which is obviously why I don't hit the bottle as often as others dear to my heart would like. From a woman's point of view I thought you only had to be very drunk – or very sorry about something and anxious to ingratiate yourself. Or, for the optimum conditions, both. I haven't seen that particular man since – something about shaking his hand at the end of the evening made me feel distinctly uncomfortable.

So if it's sound sexual certainties you're after, you're barking up the wrong babe. I blame it on marriage, myself. I've been married longer than the half-life of Caesium 137 with only a little time off for bad behaviour. And I'm not alone.

PMS Many women of my certain age are suffering from PMS – prolonged marriage syndrome. We've woken up somewhere past thirty and discovered that, lo and behold, just like Sleeping Beauty, we have lived happily ever after and now are stuck with it. Sex has become something we do once a month, or twice on holiday. It's in the contract. The handsome prince has been and gone and is now happily watching golf (the opposite of sex – the ball gets more foreplay) drinking a glass of white Bordeaux he bought from a mail-order wine club. The handsome princelings are looking for help with their homework and the royal rodents – assorted pet gerbils, hamsters and mice who are rattling around on their treadmills, laughing their minuscule balls off and asking, 'Who's in the cage, Princess?'

LOPE Alternatively the forty-something might be suffering from Late Onset Post-partum Exhaustion – like ME with babies. Her biological clock has gone off alarmingly late, leaving her a first-time mother at an age when the early starters are all grannies, a demanding job which she needs to pay the mortgage, an antipodean nanny and a child with either a worryingly strange name like Paris or Polenta to reflect her rapidly dwindling free spirit, or alternatively called something duller than Derek to make her feel posh. She is certainly not having sex. She's having hallucinations from lack of sleep and wondering how she ever fancied the child's hapless, mostly absent father.

SAD Otherwise, she has Single Anxiety Disorder. She has tick-tock, like tinnitus ringing in her ears as she calculates how many times she will ovulate before she's fifty. She feels as though she's sitting on the tombola stall during the last minutes of the jumble sale when all the tickets have already been sold. She hoards maternity catalogues and dreams of matinée jackets – and men are terrified of her because she gives off a desperate whiff of baby hormones. She can't have sex because the only men willing are other women's husbands.

Of course a lucky few are having a coital feast while we starve. They're having six courses, a side salad and chocolate truffles and we're stuck doing the dishes. But who said life was one long sexathon? It goes around, it comes around, it slows, it stops. But if you're out of practice, it's another cause of anxiety. While I'm sitting on the ride with my ticket in my hand waiting for the music, I often wonder if there's a brand new way to do it and no one has told me about it. I'm out of touch with fashion. While I was nesting and hatching chicks, chastity, apparently became the new promiscuity – with a whole generation of girls saving up all their disappointments for after they are married instead of getting a few out of the way first. Sex is now considered safe if you use a condom – on which I will comment merely by drawing your attention to two of my children – and Tantric sex the ultimate erotic experience, though it just sounds like normal sex after too much alcohol to me.

My friend Ed told me that he thought he was having a close encounter of the mystical kind when his performance was somewhat retarded after a heavy night on the booze. He could hear funny electronic noises and repeated beeping coming from the bed. He opened his eyes fearing alien abduction only to find his girlfriend playing Tetris on her Game Boy. Take your time, she said, I'm only on level three. So you see, even technology has wrought changes.

Jill Conner Browne, author of a New York Times bestseller, The Sweet Potato Queen's Book of Love, has a theory that every woman needs five men in their life – one she can talk to, one who pays for stuff, one to dance with, one to fix things for her and one for hot sex. She also maintains that four out of five can be gay. Well, I am no Sweet Potato Queen (as already mentioned, I've only had the experience of being a runner-up) but unless the sisters all die and go to live in San Francisco – I don't know why she thinks it's any easier to find a bunch of gay guys willing to accommodate you, than it is to find straight men.

Certainly, if you want a dancing partner you're going to be looking at either a gay man, a Latin American or a 60-year-old chap called Ernest who took ballroom dancing lessons at his all-male boarding school. Believe, me no straight WASPy man over 25 will budge from his seat unless he's marrying you and it's dance with the bride time – while, from my admittedly limited experience of Clubs (in Britain they're a chocolate biscuit which comes in a pack of five), all the under 25s just twitch to that throbbing sort of music that sounds like a heart monitor. There's no physical contact unless you want to give them CPR. The last time I went to a night club in New York City, the men were all getting henna tattoos on their legs and walking around gingerly for the rest of the evening like Masons, with one trouser leg rolled up, and I was the only woman in a dress – though my friend Roland looked very fetching in a sarong.

So if you discount the very young, there's a distinct possibility that your dancing partner may wear little leather pumps with Cuban heels. It's also likely that there could be some misunderstanding about who is going to be the girl. Surprise – it might not be you. Though in the case of the Latin American, any macho Mambo man worth his salsa should definitely want to lead – albeit from below with his nose pressed firmly into your cleavage. Dancing cheek to chest raises the further advantage that, properly done with a suitably sexy partner, you get an early indication of your partner's amorous intentions – always assuming you don't mistake desire for his mobile phone set on vibrate. Dancing can offer a preview of forthcoming attractions – or not – as a samba-strutting friend of mind found recently when the man she had smooched with all night appeared to have a small Bic lighter in his pocket and she then discovered he didn't smoke.

Of course gay men can also do car maintenance and yard work. My aunt's handyman Vito – an Italian American with more beef than a meatball sandwich – is an Adonis in ripped jeans. Only the fact that he has his initials embroidered across his carpenter's apron gives him away. But if a gay man is good with hammers and chisels, believe me, baby, there's a queue of Village People waiting for his services – and he can date the others standing in it. And sure, you can talk to him, but there's no point in asking him questions like, 'Do men really like it when women shave their pubic hair into a heart shape?' or 'Why do men persist in buying red underwear for Valentine's Day?' He doesn't know the answer – he isn't representative of your focus group.

That just leaves paying for stuff, which, whether the man is gay or straight, begs the question – why the hell should he? In my experience there are only two sorts of men who will indulge you financially – one is your father and the other one wants to sleep with you. It's important to know the difference.

Nevertheless, it's true that you are not going to get everything you want from one man. The perfect woman is supposedly someone who arrives naked, brings food, does laundry and is gone in the morning. And I'm sure bottle skills come into it somewhere. Women's needs are usually a little more complex.

Some of us want to be looked after, but we don't want to be mothered. Some of us want bastards who are sensitive and kind. We want cosy cuddles, cute teddy bears and rough sex with handcuffs. How can one person possibly indulge our every schizophrenic whim? As in all things, it's better to diversify. So, if you want a man who fixes stuff and your partner is a klutz, hire a handyman and pray for pecs and a very hot day. Or here's a radical thought. Do it yourself.

Taking care of your own needs

While I enjoy a man with muscles who isn't afraid of hard labour, I always feel it's rather wasted on odd jobs. Fortunately, you can pay a man to come to your home, strip down to his undershirt and get into a sweat in your bathroom just as long as, nominally at least, he is fixing your pipes. But in the absence of a man, I can happily tackle almost any job myself. Give me my Black and Decker drill with hammer action and I'm only too happy to go it alone.

As a girl, I didn't want a Tiny Tears, cry and pee dolly, I wanted my own power tool, and though I do all the traditionally girlie things like bitch, cleanse and exfoliate, underneath my push-up bra beats the heart of a big strapping chap with tattoos (though henna is for wimps), a full set of retractable spanners and a bad case of penis envy. And while other women dream of wall-to-wall carpeting, I'd rather get out my workmate, get down on the hardwood floors and set to work with a heavy-duty sander.

It all comes from being banished from the kitchen at an early age and being forced instead to follow my father while he did various manly things around the house. Well that and realising that I wasn't beauty queen material. If decoration wasn't an option open to me, then I'd better be useful I held measuring tapes and passed wrenches like a magician's assistant and as a result, learned to tackle any basic task around the house – I can cut glass, fill cavities and drill holes. I can screw anything against the wall. As with sex, I'm not imaginative, but I can follow instructions, understand diagrams and do as I'm told. Put me in a pair of overalls and a white t-shirt, give me an oil rag and a claw hammer – and there I am with the hood up and my hand fumbling around inside the engine pretending I'm an honorary bloke. If car maintenance was the Karma Sutra I'd be stripping down engines quicker than a table dancer gets down to her pom poms, but until then, I content myself by topping up the water for the windshield wipers and checking the tyre pressure.

Whenever something goes wrong around the house, I get down and dirty and attempt to fix it. This is because I am married to a man who feels that taking out the trash is the ultimate expression of masculinity. He thinks that a vacuum is a void – a space completely empty of all matter – usually because he hasn't switched the damn thing on. This leaves me free to swagger about the house in my grubby dungarees, a pencil behind my ear, waving my industrial-sized torch, playing at being the man of the house. Mind you, it's only playing. I'm certainly not the one wearing the trousers, but I do wear the pants.

Who wear the pants in your household?
Well I hope it's you, too. Not that I necessarily think that men should be walking around letting it all blow free in the breeze, but surely you can sort out your own man's underwear without any nonsense

from me — and I sincerely hope he would leave your pants alone when he's dressing in the morning. If he's slinking off to work in your thong, unless he's a cocktail waitress, I'd be worried. Enough said.

Undercover operations Relationships, just like make-up, require a good foundation and when you're looking for a little support, you've got to build from the bottom up. So, even if DIY is not your thing, in this area you should do your prep work and strip back to the basics — invest in four weeks' worth of matching froth, or if you look like me, matching underwired froth, and for gravity's sake — buy yourself a decent bra (as long as you're secure in the knowledge that you alone will be wearing it). By this I don't mean a white sports bra with cross-over straps that stop you bouncing all over the squash court. Within limits, squash is good. Think flattering, not flattening. Go to a lingerie store and have yourself kitted out in the proper uniform — something with underwire and lace, and if you still don't have enough cleavage, buy it a cup size smaller. Wearing an ill-fitting bra is very bad for your circulation, but for about 25 minutes, it's very good for your figure.

There is no getting away from the fact that underwear plays more than just a walk-on, take-off role in sex. In films, women always wear the man's shirt to cover post-prandial awkwardness — possibly the single most shapelessly unflattering garment known to curvy-hipped women. Sheets do a better cover-up job, but you look, frankly, odd walking around like a trainee bride dragging the bed behind you. Get back into your silk camisole and you're a dishevelled babe.

If you're either a mistress or a table dancer, then your lingerie can indeed be the star of your sex life. Men, apparently, love it, though to me, bras are one of the few little thrills you can enjoy alone that don't come with batteries, but then I am a simple soul with simple gift-wrapped pleasures.

I didn't wear a bra until I was 26 and pregnant for the first time. For about six months I was strutting around thinking I was Miss July in the Pirelli calendar, and then poof, they were gone until the next pregnancy. Three babies later the novelty had worn off somewhat, but not the breasts. When I went to be fitted for a new bra recently and was told my cups had runneth over I came home wearing a double D smile and a bra the same size. 'Is that good?' he asked. 'Well, just imagine if you suddenly discovered that you could measure your own equipment from the knee up and think about how you'd feel,' I replied. He'd probably run out and insure it.

So although I'm currently unavailable for active duty, I'm definitely in the sexy apparel reserves. I'm experiencing an uplifting moment every morning as I squeeze myself into my balcony bra and then sit out on it with a cup of coffee and a newspaper. So my drawers are awash with little bits of rosebud lace and gauzy black frills, each of which makes me feel as though I'm off to indulge in a cinq à sept assignation with some rich Eurotrash instead of just schlepping to the supermarket to buy bin bags.

The last thing I bought was a corset. A cantilevered, gold brocade strapless basque with a neckline that not so much plunges as leaps head first to the depths of the navel. It looks as though it should come with its own Jane Austen screenplay and a man in white hose and a curly wig especially cast to hold up the stockings. Even better, according to the fitter, it's supposed to be tight. My mother used to wear Playtex 18-hour girdles that effectively stopped her bending for about 20 years. I never thought I'd get caught in the same vice, but there you go – flab makes stomach-suckers of us all. But at least mine has frills.

However, the drawback of all this stuffing and squeezing is that it is bloody uncomfortable. There's no getting away from the fact that lace itches and stockings are ridiculous – albeit the equivalent of a baboon's bum to the male population. I don't mind a bra and a pair of matching knickers but I draw the line at stockings – firmly across the top of my thigh where they cling like leeches and make me feel like a tart on a bad thigh day.

Panting for sex Pants are another problem. You want to wear the little scraps of nothing held together by dental floss and imagination, but they seem to have been designed more for the male eye than the female body – and men don't have to suffer the string burrowing into their buttocks like they're looking for loose change down the side of a sofa. You wear them more for effect than for comfort, hoping that by the time the man actually sees your knickers the chances are you've already decided you're going to take them off.

This is why mothers always buy you extra large knickers for Christmas – it's nothing to do with the need for sensible underwear and everything to do with keeping you pure and chaste in a state of constant embarrassment. I can't really see the problem here, as if you don't want them to appear in the bedroom scene all you have to do is nip into the nearest Ladies Room, take the damn things off and stick them in your handbag. Okay, he might think you are a wanton tart, but at least not a tart with nightmare pants.

But if you're worried about pants – don't even get me started on the subject of pantie liners. How embarrassed are you going to be if he gets a highly absorbent paper towel stuck to the back of his hand? What the hell are you wearing them for anyway? Unless she's planning to shampoo carpets, no woman carries around that much pre-menstrual moisture.

Mothers get equally contrary on the subject of pants. They buy you multi-packs of one-size fits-all-elephants, 100 per cent cotton old-lady underwear with flannel gusset – a word so horrible that if they embroidered it across the front of your knickers you would never want to have sex ever again – and urge you to wear it, but only if you aren't planning on being hit by a car. Then, you stop being their daughter and magically transmogrify into Superwoman, able to

135

stop the speeding truck, milliseconds before it hits you, nip into a phone booth and change into a colour co-ordinated bra and teeny tiny matching thong, so as to impress the doctor when he's cutting them off you later looking for your spleen. Hey – he might be single. Or he could even be a she. What are you supposed to do then – hope she's a lesbian and embrace an alternative lifestyle? Well, your mum would say, I bet she has a good pension plan and a private practice.

My advice is to take the big pants, treat them like bad hairdressers, say 'lovely', then send them off to Martha Stewart so she can transform them into place mats and a matching table centrepiece. Do not use them as dusters. First – you should never, ever dust anything except talcum powder, and second – if it's embarrassing to wear the darn things, how much more humiliating is it going to be when a visitor mops up a spilt drink with a pair of outsize floral knickers?

Or you could always just hide them in a drawer and wear them when there's absolutely no chance of you meeting George Clooney at the dry cleaners – or alternatively when you tire of feeling like your bum is a round of cheddar being sliced into wedges. Believe me when I tell you – that day will come. On the big pants question I'm split, like a watermelon, and it's not a good look. So, shamed as I am to admit it, I wear mine whenever necessary.

Men are fixated either on breasts or on buttocks. Women are fixated only on the buttocks despite, or perhaps because of, our own bottom being impossible to see without eyes in the back of the head. I used to think I had a big bum until it became so prominent that if I stood too still in Central London I'd surely be declared a national landmark. Sightseeing buses would put it on their schedule of regular stops and Japanese tourists could pose beside me for photographs. Then maybe I'd start a trend and others of my kind would join me – instead of one wide-bottomed woman skulking in the big girl aisles of department stores like a man outside a sex shop, there would

be whole herds of us. In winter we'd migrate to the January
sales and we could have spring mating rituals with the men in
the Husky Hunks XXL store.

National Geographic could do a documentary on us.

But until that happy day we're isolated in the rear-view mirror,
worrying anxiously about the size of our buttocks. Truly it's not
woman's ability to bear children that marks the difference between
the sexes – it's big bum neurosis. Even skinny girls who are patently
not so afflicted, pinch handfuls of air in the place where their
phantom bottoms should be and say, 'Oooh, I'm so fat!' Does my
bum look big in this is the question on everyone's hips. Well of
course it does – we're genetically programmed to store excess fat
on the lower body and unless you are pregnant or very overweight,
your bottom is designed to be bigger than your waist. It's like a sofa
– it's supposed to be nicely upholstered and comfortable to sit on. It
is, however, not supposed to be covered in floral prints, cat hair or
antimacassars and men should not sit on you.

But what's the alternative? The Greek widow look – head-to-
toe black with accompanying hump? Polyester fat pants?
Elasticated waistbands? Tunics? Tunics are the fashion equivalent
of a wedding marquee except that instead of marrying the man
you marry the tent. So don't rush into anything. Think again.
Camouflage is not the answer. Come out of the
closet and be proud of your natural assets. Turn the
other cheek. You don't have to be a fugitive just
because your waist doesn't like publicity. Since
the average dress size is in
the double digits there
are obviously a lot of
fuller figured females
around. What's the big
secret – who are we trying
to hide it from?

I have good child-bearing
hips but child-bearing produces

convenient little hand-holds, like rock climbers use, all along the north face of the bottom. These would prove useful if a party of mountaineers ever want to scale my heights.

Otherwise I can't see the need for them.

So we must assume they are purely for decoration and act accordingly.

The male species

Victoria's really big Secret is not lingerie but the fact that men don't give a damn about the side of your bum. They are just glad that you have one. According to the *Daily Telegraph*, one in five men think that cellulite is a kind of battery. These are the ones you want to plug into.

When it comes to love, as with underwear, there is absolutely no accounting for tastes. One woman's passion is another's poison. You can wear the same style of clothes as your girlfriend, love her apartment and enjoy the same films, but deeply disapprove of, even dislike her choice of boyfriend – which is just as it should be. There are some things in life you shouldn't share – toothbrushes, used tissues, knickers and, most important of all, men.

Unadulterated love On the question of married men, I will state the obvious and say that you really shouldn't borrow another woman's husband, her life partner, her live-in lover or her significant other – even if you do intend to give him back when you're finished. Men are not library books – you should really go out and get your own copy.

Adultery is taboo, but some of us must be doing it – all those marriages don't end in divorce just because men leave the toilet seat up. But your mother will certainly not tell you she has been having an affair with the man next door – unless she is the unfortunate diagram-drawing sort who will offer to show you the pictures. Nevertheless, you never know – mothers have libidos, too, even if having married your father seems to belie it. They might have been surreptitiously flicking through the male section of the catalogue for years. Some of you will also find yourself checking out a reserved man at some time of your life, but you needn't look to me for censure – I've been to that library myself and taken out a few that I had no intention of keeping but just wanted to look at for a while. I've been divorced and yes, my ex and I did have irreconcilable differences – but they had names like Bill, Bob and George. We were already separated at the time, but I was still guilty on a technicality. I know, I know, it's not pretty and it's not nice – but this isn't *Jane Eyre*. No one goes rushing off into the night because they discover the object of their affections has a mad wife hiding in the attic. These days the other woman lights the fire herself.

Am I your conscience here? Good God, no – people get tired of marriage. They get tired of each other. There are no guarantees in life and you don't get your money back if you decide you don't like it. But cheating is a messy business and it's going to corrode your soul.

The married man is either disappointed or greedy. He either loves his wife and doesn't want to leave her or doesn't love her enough to pay maintenance. He wants to supplement his income. He loves his children, but he likes sex with you better than bedtime stories with them. And he wants to be honest with you – he just doesn't want to give you his home telephone number.

You're on a long hike to nowhere but Christmas, Thanksgiving and birthdays (if they fall on a weekend) spent back at your mother's and Sunday afternoons sitting alone in the launderette watching your small life spin round waiting for the whispered phone call. Whether the adulterer or the adulteree you are entering a world of deceit, cell phones and non-existent dog-walking. You won't like yourself and if you think about what's involved you won't like him either. If he tells you his wife doesn't understand him – well, of course she doesn't. He's lying to her about the time he spends with you, he's a duplicitous snake who wants to have his cake, eat it, admire it and eat it again tomorrow – what's to understand?

Try particularly hard to avoid the good liar: the serial adulterer who has a Tuesday night slot (a boring business dinner), a free Friday afternoon (when he's supposedly playing golf) and who gives you an appointment card. Remember that a man who is so practised in compartmentalising his life that he can keep all his balls in the air and catch them in different baskets can hardly be relied on to tell you alone the whole truth. Anyone who has ever cheated knows the stomach-curdling awfulness of looking straight into the eyes of a person, to whom you have once professed love, and lying. Being the deceived wife is even worse – we all know what it feels like to be lied to. You can't just switch sides because you don't like the team you're on. And if you're both married then you're joined by your mutual infidelities – well at least you have something else in common apart from sex.

Men are usually spectacularly bad liars, so most of the innocent will be alerted early on. Men leave their mobile phones lying around and let you read their lover's text messages. They print out their illicit e-mails and let you pay the credit card bills for hotels you've never stayed in. They take out the library books and ask you to return them and pay all the fines. And they borrow really bad titles – *Pigs in Lipstick*, *The Joy of Secretaries*, *The Babysitter's Club* and *Alimony*.

But enough. In a past life I used to be a librarian. Aged seventeen I stole a book, packed it in my suitcase and left home with it. Even though I sent it back anonymously some time later I have dust on my hands. So we'll have silence on the subject and anyone who wants to discuss it further can see me outside. Later.

The short lover If you've been having trouble with unfaithful partners maybe you're not choosing the right man — maybe you aren't looking at the right altitude, never mind wavelength. The short man is an undervalued quantity — a much-maligned species often passed over for his more macho big brother.

According to a study of a group of men who graduated in 1950 from the US military academy at West Point, the secret of a successful, long married life is to marry beneath you. Taller men tend to have more children, with more partners, and are more likely to be unfaithful, get divorced and remarry. But don't get excited and start scouring the small ads for Little Big Man — remember that the men in this study are now septuagenarians. A lot has changed since 1950 — it could be that the women who were originally married to the West Pointers just got fed up being barked at like raw recruits, and asked for an honourable discharge.

But the tall, dark, handsome men of cliché are deemed to be more attractive, powerful and masculine than their vertically challenged brothers. Consequently we women are supposedly falling over our high heels to get into their genes. Growing up in a country where half the male population seemed to be under five foot, I have a bit of a height complex. I'm not particularly tall, but adolescence in the land of knuckle-dragging midgets has left me with an overly inflated idea of my own stature — being cast as a boy in country dancing lessons because you're the tallest in the class will do that sort of thing to you.

It's also true that as an averagely tall woman with matching husband, I always thought that in my next life it would be nice to be married to someone whose diminutive relatives weren't introduced to my breasts two weeks before they met the rest of me. A man I could dance with and not have my head bobbing over his shoulder like a horse at the paddock door. A man I could look up to, whom I could lean on without knocking him over, and whose mother didn't greet me with unabashed glee simply because I can reach objects on a high shelf.

Most men lie about their age, their marital status or how many women they've slept with, but initially my husband lied about his height. So smitten with love and lust was I that I believed in those few extra inches. I trusted him, though I still spent the early years of our courtship gazing at our reflection in shop windows just to make sure he had the edge, and wore flat shoes for a decade as extra insurance. That we're still married would certainly give credence to the argument that relationships with short men can be constant. However, the cost of divorce might have something to do with it. Twin mortgages and child support are expensive. Tall men may father more children, but that's the easy, fun part where everyone's the same height lying down. But in today's economic climate it's paying for the kids that separates the men from the boys, not their inside leg measurement. You need lofty ambitions and a salary to match to play at pick and mix dysfunctional families.

However, I can't deny the allure of a tall man. My father was six foot two and the only man in my life who I've ever been able to look up to – and stand on my tip-toes to kiss. Well, on a regular basis at least. But although being tall may be desirable, it's still not enough to transform a man into a babe magnet. Height, or the lack of it, doesn't make you more faithful or more appealing. Nevertheless, tall men don't feel they have to try so hard in the desirability stakes – almost as if hitting your head on the door frame was a positive personality trait. This does not always make them the best life partners – and it plays havoc with the paintwork. They also take up more room in the bed and, given that all men seem genetically unable to sit with their knees together, when they sit next to you on trains, planes and automobiles they annex most of your space and crush your legs.

At the low end of the scale, we've all met the chap with a bad case of small man syndrome who tries to make up with attitude what he lacks for in inches. But you don't marry them, unless you're Nicole Kidman or Demi Moore. The sensible, sexy short man is not ripping his shirt off like Sylvester Stallone pretending to be Rambo, he's turning on the charm or making you laugh. You could argue that a shorter man who is funny, eager to please and eager to prove himself is going to attract more female attention and therefore more likely to stray. If he doesn't marry as often as the tall guy it's because his wife is not inclined to let him trot off and amuse someone else.

The further advantage of marrying down and having the courage to wear heels and be damned, is that you comfort yourself with the fantasy that onlookers, instead of thinking, God, look at that shortarse with that Amazonian woman, will merely imagine that he is rich. If the man in question also happens to be bald, then they'll think he's very, very rich. Or as a woman I met at a party recently whispered while my husband was up at the bar getting drinks – I bet he's very good in bed.

Well, I was hardly going to contradict her, was I?

The bald lover Baldness is disguised vanity, but a healthier and more attractive vanity than swirling the remaining hair on top of their head like a Mr Whippy cone. Bald men are brave. They have grasped the fact that their hair is falling out as they catch it in the hairbrush every morning and dared to be bare. They have shaved it off and toughed it out. They have guts where other men have receding hairlines and bad combovers.

There are two kinds of bald men – the fat bald man and the firm bald man. The fat bald man has probably lost his hair slowly and inevitably. He has a sports car, two mobile phones and a lot of keys. The firm bald man has hit the razor and the gym at the same time. He knows he has to make the best of what he has left – and this isn't going to be attained by growing a pony tail from a circle of hair at the nape of his neck. Pecs – yes, plaits – no.

But bald and beautiful is a tricky one to pull off – two much white scalp and the guy risks looking as if he's suffering from a horrible illness, though it's always easy to spot him in a crowd. Too much oil and he looks like a billiard ball. Too much stubble gives you razor burn in places that are difficult to get sympathy for – plus stubble is the ghost of Christmas past and shows how little new growth you have. At least the all over slaphead look leaves the fiction that he could grow it back if he wanted it.

Bald men are to be encouraged. They have seen the future and put on leather coats and dark glasses. And as men embrace grooming like it's a naked blonde in a fur coat, we don't need them cluttering up the hairdressers. Plus you can always borrow their razors.

The e-mail lover Nearly everyone I know has had an e-mail flirtation. It's not hard to see why – you have the time, the inclination and the opportunity – all you need is an e-mail account and the virtual world's your oyster. Most people have access to e-mail at work, where they fondly imagine their correspondence to be private – it only takes an office memo with a hint of innuendo and you're all set for a bit of on-line chatting up.

It's all so instant. You type a sassy reply but unlike normal correspondence you don't have time to reconsider while the letter languishes on the hall table waiting for the annual visit to the letterbox.

Instead of looking at its naked, stampless exterior wondering if it was wise to tell your room-mate at college that you slept with her boyfriend, or to ask the chap at the next desk about the size of his mailbox, with e-mail it's too late – it's already gone.

By the time you've logged off the ex-room mate has already spread the news amongst a dozen of her very close friends – who in turn have forwarded your message to every bulletin board in cyberspace – and she's sent you a reply calling you a promiscuous slut. Meanwhile, your in-tray is surging with byte-sized messages from the chap at the next desk and you've got male, and a date in real-time later that evening.

E-mail positively begs for shared confidences and unwise confessions. Like praying, you sit there and commune with your keyboard, formulating your innermost thoughts and desires before sending them off into the ether to a benevolent God substitute who, unlike the real thing, eventually answers. For a while, every time I clicked the queue button on my mail box I felt like a little kid at Christmas sending my wish list up the chimney, but instead of watching my heartfelt desires burn to a crisp, they were whisked away and, if not granted, then at least favourably received. I didn't get a Sindy Dream House with fully fitted kitchen, but neither did I get a box of day of the week panties and a pair of flannelette pyjamas.

E-mail forces you to use your imagination and we all know that reality is rarely as obliging as the picture you conjure up in your mind. Experience ranges from the widespread one-handed typing of chat rooms to finding your once-in-a-lifetime true soulmate who impresses you with his personality and his prose style. If you are to believe everything you read on screen, then half of America's armed forces are indulging in e-mail adultery when they should be defending the nation; all IT workers are living parallel lives as sex gods instead of manning their helplines; and bored housewives are a lot less bored than they pretend. Disillusion often follows once you discover that the Puerto Rican musician who calls you 'mi corazón' is really a 76-year-old grandfather from

Boondocks, Alabama, and lives on social security, and that the man at the next desk was exaggerating about the size of his stapler – in cyberspace everyone's a size 10 staple. And sooner or later you will have to 'fess up that you are not a 23-year-old lingerie model studying neurosurgery at Harvard. Be prepared for virtual disappointment.

The World Wide Web is a tangled one to navigate if you try to spin it too far. It's difficult to remember all your separate identities, far less the passwords and security codes you need to protect your various internet accounts. I have so many different PINs for everything from banking, credit cards, savings and e-mail that I can hardly keep track of them. If you want to practise e-mail sex you have to have a very good memory.

You also have to be prepared to be fired when your boss discovers you've been misusing your office e-mail.

I admit that not only have I been there, I have seen the movie, got the t-shirt and eaten the happy meal at MacDonalds, having once stumbled inadvertently into a chaste flirtation with an e-mail soul mate who turned out to live not ten minutes away from my house. We could have skipped the technology and communicated with two tin cans and a length of string.

Worryingly, he also wore cowboy boots and clothes with little alligators on the chest, had a wife, two children – and still thinks my name is Allison, which is as much as I'm willing to divulge.

The virtual lover By this I don't mean the one who exists in cyberspace, I mean the one you do virtually everything with except have sex. It's an immaculate affair. You flirt, you flatter, you talk endlessly and intimately but you don't sleep together. Some women do allow a bit of extra-curricular kissing, but I'd say you're playing with fire there and it's going to spread up your arm, down your body and into the other parts you really don't want to reach.

I met a couple of men at a party recently who told me how much they enjoyed cooking. 'But we have to say that,' added one, 'it's what you do if you want to get laid – like having a motorbike used to be'. 'It wouldn't work for me,' I confided. Being a little bit sad, a little bit desperate and very easily pleased (not to mention very, very married) – I'd go for flattery every time. The problem is that there comes a time when men start telling you they love you for your mind, not your body. They say you're 'interesting', or 'How nice it is to meet someone who has a brain', while wearing a drop-dead-gorgeous blonde bimbette draped across their arm.

Oh gee, that makes you feel just dandy. When men start congratulating you on how unexpectedly 'interesting' you are, you suddenly get a great desire for them to look at your breasts.

Now the virtual lover will do both. He'll ogle your body, tell you that you should be running the Foreign Office, admire your dress, your cleavage, your perfume, ask your opinion on his love life and cook for you. Hell, he'll even buy you dinner and it's free of any sexual price tag.

He's a walker, a safe bet, a friend whom you fancy but will never fondle, except accidentally on purpose as you brush your hand against his reaching for your wine glass. He applauds your successes and glosses over your failures. He makes you giggle. He laughs at your sparkling wit. When you're together you're Dorothy Parker and he's Woody Allen but taller and with more hair. You talk endlessly about sex – and this is the man to reassure you when you have matters of pressing urgency to discuss such as 'Why do men like stockings?' and 'Is fat really a feminist issue or does it bother men too?' You'll get a just about easy-to-bear honest answer, sex tips and complete, unabridged dispatches from behind the enemy lines. If you ask your girlfriend why the current object of your affections hasn't called you in a week, she will probably say he has forgotten your number, the virtual lover will tell you to give it up – the creep has dumped you and you'll never hear from him again. And somehow when he adds, with suitable sincerity, that the man in question doesn't know a good thing when he sees it, you feel truly comforted. He's always on your good side and you know you can bask in his continued appreciation.

It's the almost perfect relationship – as long as you never sleep together. With the virtual lover you will never get home having lost your underpants in the taxi. You will never be tempted to slip off to the Ladies Room in a bar, train, plane or restaurant while he's in there waiting for you. He won't give you razor burn, carpet burn, bruises on your arms, scratches on your back or love bites that you need to explain the next morning. This, of course, raises its own problems. If he isn't sleeping with you, he's sleeping with someone else. Eventually he'll fall in love with the someone else and the virtual affair is virtually over. You'll be demoted to the junior ranks of the ex-fancied. No more cosy lunches. No more brief encounters over the dinner table. No more mutual appreciation society with gratuitous sexual Fresno.

But you'll still have your memories. And the restraining order slapped on you by his new girlfriend who doesn't want you anywhere within three miles of him.

But it was nice while it lasted.

The young lover I know a few women who've gone out with younger men – some have even married them – but not a lot of the mothers outside school admit that they're secretly sleeping with a sixth former. But somebody must be doing it. So many men have told me, eyes a-glowing with fond remembrance, that their first time was with an older woman. So unless the same one has been very, very busy, there's something my friends aren't telling me.

Of course there's no denying the charms of an 18-year-old boy with long, lean limbs and unfunny, unfixed muscles, but I can't forget that these lads are other women's sons. I have two boys of my own and that's not the sort of private education I want for them.

Young men are prized for their energy, but since women these days are starting their families later and later, it's difficult to see how a woman with an infant on one hip could be bothered with an even bigger infant groping for her breast. Young men are also incredibly eager and – let's not forget – fast. I'd rather travel once and get there than stop and start a hundred times for rest and recuperation. It's also hard enough to train a fully mature male to do complicated seek-and-find tasks like where their own socks are or how to programme the video-recorder, without setting up a course on carnal knowledge. And yes, young men have the stamina to stay up all night, but if it's a school night and you have to make them a packed lunch the next morning – is it worth it? Admittedly the homework might be fun but none of the men I knew in my twenties were that good at geography – I doubt much has changed.

But a friend of mine who recently discovered the joys of non-conjugal sex after the break-up of her marriage says you simply don't have any choice but to take up with a younger man. Men her own age aren't interested. Men her own age are put off by three things – dependent children, fours with zeros unless they're inside your bra, and underarm hair. Luckily you can shave off all three – at least until the alarm goes off next morning.

Age used to be venerated, but nowadays we save our admiration for those who think prolapsed is an anti-depressant. However, according to my friend, age does have its compensation. God is on the side of women who've had it all and don't want any more of it thank you.

Young men have attitude and long hair – and they have the further advantage of being terrified of women their own age. The sultry girl in the spaghetti-strap dress who you think would be winding them around her fork is squandering her youth looking for commitment. She sees blokes her own age as potential baby-making material – she checks out his body for good chromosomes, his wallet for six months maternity leave and his teeth to make sure he still has them all. So the slightly older woman is a life-jacket, fully inflated and bobbing on a sea of non-commitment, offering recreational sex without rings.

I suppose you had better save the poor bugger before he drowns. But let him make his own packed lunch, for goodness sake. And teach him good bedroom manners.

The ex-lover The ex-lover hangs around your sitting room like the ghosts in *Truly, Madly, Deeply*, though they don't do anything as innocuous as watch TV. Instead they stare at you from the sofa where they once smoked a cigarette and told you they were leaving. When you look at the walls where their posters once hung you can still see the empty spaces and the naked picture hooks, although they've been covered with polyfilla and paint for years.

These ghosts lie around house like sleeping dogs who have to be kicked out of the way every now and again so you can get on with your life. They whine at the end of the non-ringing phones and whimper piteously when you check your phantom e-mail. They scratch at doors which you steadfastly refuse to open – and they stink. They fill the rooms with the smell of disappointment and the odd sour scent of happier times gone wrong. But these ghosts, at least, you learn to ignore. You co-exist until they fade into the pattern of the wallpaper. Oh you, you lying, cheating, egotistical shit, move out the way so I can sit down at the table. What did I ever see in you anyway? Ugly brute.

Eventually you do a spot of emotional spring cleaning. Feng Shui for failed romance. You rearrange the furniture, change the bed, redecorate. You bring a new body home to exorcise the others – though you know he's only looking round, sizing the place up and finding a nice comfortable spot to drop his baggage. All the better to repossess you when it's over.

But in the outside world, these ghosts roam free. You can see them, with versions of your younger self, hanging around street corners like aimless teenagers, quarrelling in restaurants, crying in cabs – sometimes laughing so hard that you can still join in the joke, years later. You can go back and visit the past like the Stations of the Cross. The place where you got married, the place where you filed for divorce. The bedsit, the flat, the hovel, the table in the restaurant where you fell in love.

But sorrow fades eventually like a cheap perfume. One day you just can't smell it any more. And you start again.

The ghosts can always use company.

The romantic lover is exactly like the virtual lover, except that this time you also get the hot sex. You get flowers. You get sentimental trinkets. You get books and CDs and full-on flattery which he apparently believes. He takes you out for dinner and will never let you split the bill. He thinks that you're Aphrodite, he's a god in bed. He remembers your two-month anniversary. He calls – but not too much – and is usually available – but not too often. He is never late for a date and always waiting for you at the airport. He thinks you're beautiful and insists your freckles are cute. He loves round women. He thinks you have the intellect of Einstein and that your mother is Stalin – but only when you're cross with her... Most of the time he likes your mother, even when she's on sabbatical, training the Vietcong in torture techniques, because he wants her for a mother-in-law. The romantic lover is a keeper. He wants your babies. He wants to marry you on the beach in Bali.

He brushes his teeth before he kisses you in the morning and cleans out the washbasin afterwards. He doesn't wear socks and so naturally can't sleep in them, his fingernails are self-trimming and he has a genetic inability to belch. He doesn't use a toothpick when you're anywhere within ten miles of him and he flosses, in private.

His only drawback is that you can't ask him for advice on how to seduce other men. Nor can you ever discuss your previous sexual partners, the quantity, the quality and the fact that they are still hiding in the wardrobe. The chances are that he's still 'friends'

151

with his ex-girlfriend, who secretly remains in love with him, and he's on very good terms with his ex-wife. He goes round and clears her driveway when it snows and probably remembers her anniversary as well.

Well, nobody's perfect.

The dream lover Vodka and chat will keep me up after twelve, but whenever I am in sight of bed, I fall into it. I love sleep. Beautiful, dream-filled oblivion where I close my eyes and enter my own private world in which I am Queen, Empress, Supreme Deity and brutal dictator of everything that surrounds me. I can rearrange my life so that no one cries, so that none of the fabric of my life is disturbed, but still, miraculously, I can have whatever I want, at no cost. Men will fall in love with me. I have sex with strangers, some of whom I have never met in real life. I kiss the dead and scream at the living, annoyed when they turn up in my dreams, but never so much as call when I'm awake.

In sleep Russell Crowe knows my name, Pierce Brosnan calls me darling and Keanu Reeves is my love child. My stomach is firm, my thighs are smooth. My face rejuvenates. My deadlines are met and my prose profound, the dishes wash themselves and money appears, as if by magic, in my bank account. I have legs to die for and every single pair of Prada shoes ever designed. My kids grow straight teeth, score goals in every soccer match and never need help with their homework. They say, 'Oh, Mum, you run along to the opening of [insert fab night spot here] and don't worry about combing my head for nits, or finding me clean sports kit at two seconds' notice. They never ask for a costume at midnight for 'dress as your favourite book character' next day at school and I never reply by telling them to sod off. The dream me jumps up and sews one – on the spot – and the child wins first prize. There's world peace. England for the Ashes. No athletes' foot. No fungal infections or feminine itching and the toilet seat is always down. It's Marionworld, a twilight theme park of wish-fulfilment, and welcome to it.

This is where all the perfect men are – in your dreams. They don't live out there in the waking world. Men don't come with a set of instructions, and batteries aren't included. You have to work out how to use them all by yourself. The real ones, the almost perfect, are lying beside you, no doubt dreaming about Julia Roberts or the girl in the Post Office who sold them stamps that morning. If you want perfect you're looking on the wrong planet, unless you want to consider maybe your father – though if your mother's divorced you can scrub that one too. And if you don't like it then you can always stay single.

It's an option worth considering before you buy a blow-up man and install him in the passenger seat of your car. Or be like Barbie and find yourself the ultimate toyboy.

The toyboy Unlike Eve, who was created especially for Adam, in the case of Barbie and Ken the babe came first. She celebrated her 40th birthday a couple of years ago, but Ken sprang fully formed from the production line with his pre-cast buns of plastic, nothing between his ears and perplexingly little between his legs, more than two years later.

Love them or hate them, no one can deny that in marketing terms, Ken and Barbie are the model couple. They've been married continually, often in fairy-tale fashion, but only ever to each other. We have yet to see the Broken Home Barbie or Divorced Ken celebration set. Sex and kissing apart (Ken's lips are firmly shut on the subject), they seem to do everything together – surf, swim, ride bicycles and roller blade. Barbie even loves Ken enough to let him drive her car. However, though it might be every macho man's dream to chauffeur a plastic blonde around in a convertible, I can't imagine that pink would be his colour of choice for the bodywork. An engine would also be useful.

In other respects Ken is a bit of a wimp. He always moves in with Barbie and never has his own place. He puts up with her kitsch taste in furniture and seems to have no friends of his own. He doesn't even have a job.

Sadly, even though they may appear to have the ideal marriage our Barb has yet to become pregnant. It can't be that she doesn't want children, as she seems to have more infant accessories than other women have shoes. She is forever babysitting her little sister Krissy and sundry other younger siblings, sometimes in multiples of three. Surely at 42 her non-biodegradable clock must be driving every pre-pubescent girl in the country mad? But, since neither she nor Ken has the necessary equipment, adopting Chinese triplets is probably the only answer.

With the helmet hair and no nether regions, who knows what Barbie sees in Ken – but then I did miss out on her formative years due to an early attachment to her less glamorous British cousin Sindy and her constant escort Paul. My mother thought Barbie was a tart while Sindy was a nice girl. Barbie came with painted-on blue eyeshadow and no knickers, but all I remember Sindy having was a headache and a duffel coat. I'm sure by now sensible Sindy has five kids, lives in New York and has trained as a psychotherapist.

Meanwhile Ken must be facing a tough mid-life crisis. None of the Stepford sisterhood of Barbies currently residing in my kids' pink Barbie Dream Palace will ever give him house room. When Shaving Ken, complete with designer stubble, arrived on the market, he was banished to a studio apartment – a shoebox under the bed – every night. Frankly, I don't think that Safe-sex Ken could get lucky if he brought his own condoms in a diamanté case with butterfly decal.

Action Man has been living it large in our Barbie house for years. Baywatch Barbie lost her head in a skirmish during which Action Man abseiled on to the sun terrace from the heights of my son's bunk bed, thus becoming another hapless statistic of domestic violence, as well as the ultimate male fantasy. She now lies headless and helplessly available for sex on the pink plastic dream bed with matching satin sheets, while Action Man struts around the place in combat fatigues, being served miniature food on pink plates by a harem of unsuitably attired blonde clones. Ken, I'm afraid, is looking at being down-sized with only his polyester leisure wear to keep him warm.

In the real world it wouldn't work like this. He would be shaving his head and running off with one of her trophy teenage friends like Skipper, Nikki or Courtney, reading *Men's Health* and getting a tattoo. He'd be stuffing enough coke up his nose to send the whole population of Colombia to Eton, while simultaneously cutting out red meat to avoid toxins. However, with that face, at least he wouldn't have to think about Botox, and he'd never have to examine his balls.

Meanwhile, Barbie would be in therapy (as Sindy's patient), worried because Action Man won't commit, anxious that her rewarding career as Barbie dentist, dog handler or pet beautician wasn't as fulfilling as it once was – doing IVF and taking whatever the plastic equivalent of Prozac is.

But, comeawn – we all know it's a front. We all know that Ken must be gay. Look at the evidence – a four-decade fascination with flowers, dinner sets and soft furnishings. Okay, the fashion sense lets him down, but it's a foregone conclusion that he's obsessively neat, buys *GQ* – just for the articles – and definitely wears pyjamas. He keeps kitties instead of kiddies, sings show tunes and is obsessed with the kitchen. Even Barbie should know that by the time they get to 40 all the best guys are either married or gay.

And that's why little girls play with dolls.

The ones you wish you hadn't slept with Just before my friend got married she told her husband that she hoped he had no political ambitions because her personal life would not stand up to that kind of scrutiny. Luckily he was content with obscurity and her secrets never made it on to the front of the *National Enquirer*. Who wants the tabloid-reading world to find out that the entire back row of the photographed class of '82 made their inept way through your halls of residence? The artist Tracey Emin may be quite comfortable embroidering the name of every man she ever slept with on the inside of her little tent, but some women would need a marquee to accommodate their lovers, while others, rather embarrassingly, could make do with a monogrammed pocket handkerchief.

Naturally, after two weddings, frequent visits to the library and several virgin births, I fall somewhere between the hanky and a small sunhat, but nevertheless I fear that some of my neatly embroidered names would demand to be unpicked. The idea of being splashed all over the paper having people you don't know comment on your lack of morality and bad taste in men is deeply uncomfortable – as is your elementary school teacher saying you have head lice, your dentist discussing the poor quality of your bridgework or your hairdresser confirming that no, you are not a natural blonde.

But all this fades into insignificance at the idea of someone from your past downright denying that they even know you. I fear that if I become famous none of the men I have slept with will admit it. Not that many of them were such great prizes themselves, but they all shared the defining characteristic of fancying themselves rather more than they fancied me.

The Judas sleeps with you and pretends it doesn't count because you kept your clothes on, did it standing up or he had his eyes closed. He thinks getting you down on your knees is a favour – to you. He kisses you at a party and then ignores you. He takes you home from a party and says afterwards that he can't remember anything about the evening. He moves in with you merely because he has builders in his place. He marries you but says he never really loved you. He says he told you right from the start that he wasn't looking for a relationship.

He says he lost your mobile number. He says you aren't in the phone book. He says he called you but you weren't home, though you've been in bed with the phone for a month. He says, 'I'm sooo sorry, erm, erm, what did you say your name was?'

The commitment-phobe The phobic does tell you right from the start that he doesn't want a relationship. He doesn't even want to commit to lunch and breakfast – forget about it. The

phobic leaves before the wet patch on the sheet is dry. He's rung for a taxi before he has even taken your clothes off and disappears in the middle of the night when you think he's only gone to the bathroom. He doesn't want to get tied down, unless it's with your tights on the bedpost and even then you need to make very loose knots. Being tied down can mean everything from asking him his name to making a date for the following week. He won't meet your mother or accompany you to a friend's wedding. He thinks matrimony is catching – like athletes' foot – which is presumably why he makes love in his socks. Though it could also be so that he can leave quicker when it's all over. The same reason he always wears slip-on shoes.

He never makes a date, but calls up at the last minute expecting you to be free. He is invariably late for every appointment, just to keep you permanently on your toes. He doesn't believe in birthday cards and lets you buy the wine when you go to a dinner party. He doesn't share his cigarettes and likes to split the restaurant bill. He will blow you off for a sports fixture, a televised football match and a night out with his friends – but not in bed.

He says he'll call.

Sometime.

Maybe.

The cigar smoker Well, you have to kiss him eventually.

The man who gave you more than you bargained for which involved a three-week course of antibiotics.

The turncoat who broke up with you after three weeks spent tracking across China, listening to him whine about the food, his feet and his flat lifeless hair, who then decided, after long reflection in the only mirror, that he really preferred men.

The bastard makes you feel like Cleobloodypatra Queen of Denial (it's an old joke but a good one), ready to nip yourself in the asp for letting him get under your skin. He's the kind of man who keeps you smouldering in sexual suspense. Meeting him is like being involved in a traffic accident and leaves you feeling as though you've been caught in a head-on collision – but you're always the only one hurt. He walks away from the wreck unscathed.

He calls you the day after your first date, a beat after you've wondered if you'll ever hear from him again, and he gives great phone. His voice is like coffee, a slow dark-roast, velvet-smooth, double-espresso growl. When he talks, his voice drags you by the hair and pulls you across the floor on your knees, but it doesn't hurt. He breathes sex. He tells you he wants to get inside you – he wants to set up a little altar to your body, and pour libations for you. He kisses you like he wants to climb into your skin. He calls you three times a day, just to hear your voice. He sends you e-mails which pop up on your screen in the middle of conference calls which make you catch your breath with sudden lust. He strips your soul like a Russian doll, right down to the little teeny tiny one which he cracks. He takes you away for the weekend. He makes you breakfast in bed. He holds out hoops and you jump through them. He takes your heart to the top of the Empire State Building, and while you're standing there admiring the view, he gives you a shove and watches you fall.

But you can't believe it. Not the guy of the sixteen thousand sexy e-mails and the continual phone calls. He says he'll get right back to you, and you watch the phone for hours but it never rings. You start calling yourself up on your mobile just to make sure the line still works. You redirect your voice mail. You put your answerphone on twelve rings so you can get to it in time. Four days later, the message slowly dawns – he isn't calling. But still, you have faith. After what he said. After the way he acted. You call. He's never at his desk. You think, if only you could see him, you could get some sense out of the whole thing. He won't see you. It would be 'difficult', he says. And if

you run into him by accident, his cold eyes dart all over the place like he has Attention Deficit Disorder of the eyeballs. He looks over your left shoulder and smiles at another woman. Face it – the man has left the building. The altar is abandoned. He's more over than flares – he's not coming back.

Men like this should have their own website, badboyfriends.com, where we can name and shame them and alert other women to their loathsomeness. Why do they do it? It's a mystery – like why salmon swim upstream and eels migrate to the Sargasso Sea. You can't reason it out – some men are just toads in suits and there's no point in asking me why they act the way they do. I don't know either.

What am I – your mother?